The Brand and I
Kevin Green

"I haven't heard from him for two years. If I don't get a letter from him next year, I shall think of sending him one the year after."

Thomas Jefferson, talking about his Ambassador to Paris

"Perceptions shape decisions."

Perspective

This is a challenging book. There is a need to explain why many people in brand, marketing, and communications businesses believe they are 'doing the right thing', but they are still losing volume, profit, and share – and what to do to change this position profitably.

Take the case of a Marketing Director charged with improving the fortunes of a very big old food brand. He assiduously followed all the golden rules of marketing, was extremely focused, disciplined and consistent in his approach to communications, and after two years was rewarded with dramatically improved brand image and attitudes according to all his market research data. "Why, when we've done everything by the book" he asked, "don't I see any improvement in my sales performance?"

We will concentrate on two things in addressing this kind of question:

- *The costly disconnection between subjectivity and effectiveness*

- *The contribution of simplification to marketing success.*

We will look at how brands are defined and used, and take a realistic look at what should be done with many of them that is not being done today. We will look at the profound influence high levels of subjectivity have on brand destiny, which often go unrecorded in retrospective case studies. We look at how that influence is often based on distorted or diffracted personal perceptions, and often misappropriated ego over objective data and analysis. Lastly we look at what can be done with an understanding of this significant impact on brand fortunes, to improve the response to the kinds of dilemma noted here.

Subjective perceptions shape decisions. The distortions of different lenses pose a real threat to many of the challenges of achieving sustained business success. These are not simply the effects of individuals, but the cumulative effects of perspectives from new and emerging media and communication channels, like social networks. A former client, when posed with a big competitive entry into his market, organised a workshop to try to imagine what that competitor might do. The worst case scenario had the competitor cutting the price of his brand by 20–25%, with everything else merrily rolling along. The reality was much worse. The competitor dropped his price point by 50%, seriously damaging the client's business in the short term. It was beyond everyone's worst nightmare, because it was something that the client's culture, and the vision of its senior managers at the time, collectively and individually, could never have considered.

There are demonstrations of how current 'best practice' has been derived from models and behaviour that are often lagging new and challenging issues. Like in the military world, from which marketing has borrowed so much over time, many senior managers, like generals, get trapped fighting the last war, not the current or emerging one.

There is a need to challenge some of the inadequacies of the ways in which many brands are still shaped, and a need to question the value and sustainability of success based either on ageing models of idea generation between corporations, companies, creative agents and their supporting services, or on the inappropriate use of new media for many brands.

Today, there is a gap between the scientific excellence of marketing portrayed in many textbooks, and the reality in marketing communities every day. By acknowledging the ways brands, their owners, and their users really behave, and by showing how different approaches to managing brand destinies in this open-eyed world can reduce waste and improve rewards, there is here a timely and practical guide to action for anyone who has to get more value out of scarce resources, in shorter timeframes, competitively, today.

Like any work that challenges received wisdom, one can expect to hear howls of protest from those locked into and rewarded by long lasting faiths in old models of brand marketing and communication practices.

This approach is designed to give people a better chance of being realistic about brand/user models and behaviour today. This means examining what can be done to improve the form and content of highly subjective influences on brands. Too many people record brand history as though it has been a major scientific, almost clinical pursuit. Brand development is significantly more subject to individual influence than that, and learning how to manage that reality can lead to more

6

realistic performance expectations and results. The aim is to show how the appropriate management of perceptions can enhance value, as opposed to slowing down progress in a cloud of unmanaged subjectivity.

As Schopenhauer said of science, and what is equally true in the world of commerce:

"All truth passes through three stages. First, it is ridiculed. Second, it is violently opposed. Third, it is accepted as being self-evident."

About the Author

Kevin Green

After Cambridge University in the UK, Kevin spent time in global communication agencies, working across a range of clients in fast moving consumer goods, with high-tech companies, and in service industries. This provided one facet of his understanding of outside-in service-based business. He worked subsequently within a large global electronics company, providing inside-out services. He has also worked in the public sector, and has played a number of roles as a consultant, both to developing businesses and in helping people in their career development.

These roles enabled him to gain broad experience of working in significantly different types of organisations, operating cultures, and countries, with a deep respect for what can be harnessed to help people get effective results in a world with increasing demands on time and resource. The thoughts and recommendations contained here are the pragmatic distillation of many assignments, and are directed at helping people release more value from over-complex scenarios, as well as add relevant value to brands and services.

This book came to life through the realisation that for many businesses today, the approaches to marketing and communications that have evolved over the last forty years are no longer sufficiently able to support the emerging needs of brands, their managements, or their supporting service organisations. The pragmatic experiences of a key number of people, distilled by the author, and how these can translate into more relevant and valuable solutions today, are the core of the empirical supports to the book's approach.

These perspectives are there to be shared with everyone 'out there' who is doing all that can be done to get things right but is still facing major challenges. It is just possible that some adjustments in the way things are perceived and acted upon may lead to more satisfying results and fewer costly frustrations. There is an enterprise to help those wanting to spend more time learning to get more out of what they manage and serve, based on some of this thinking, and the approach is summarised at: <www.thebrandobservatory.com>.

This book and its contents are the result of working with many brands and all those who have owned, managed, lived with, worked on, and used them. There are many people who have helped shape the perspectives. Some have made me laugh, some have made me frustrated, some have been geniuses, others bullies – a rich pageant. To all of you, thank you for the experiences. To those continuing the journey, I hope the thoughts here will make the trip even more interesting and rewarding.

Contents

Book Structure

The structure creates the basis for how to get more out of the ways brands can deliver value. We look at key drivers of brand manager and brand owner behaviour that have led to many of the shortfalls and disappointments in expectations we see today. Then we look at what can be done to improve matters, profitably. Key to this is a fight against the fetish for complexity so many seem to find comfort in these days.

There is a need for a fresh perspective on what's really going on. This can unlock ways to make substantial improvements on brand investment value, returns and brand destiny.

We introduce the idea of how people have impacts on brands and their development that are different from ways that are usually discussed or recorded. There are significant implications for people who believe that brands can be managed to some higher order of scientific objectivity and rational truth. Subjectivity needs to be managed more effectively, not dismissed. We look at how old social, cultural and behavioural legacies still have major effects on current brand user and brand owner behaviour, attitudes, and perspectives. We examine how views on brand management and development get distorted, and what that means for those who are going to be charged with delivering value from the brands and businesses they are about to manage.

Part One

The Branded World and How I Made It So

1.   It's More Subjective Than You Might Think

Here we introduce the topic of how brand owners, managers, service providers, and others have profound effects on brand destinies in ways which are often unrecorded in case studies and business school classrooms. It is the reality of how brands are shaped, as opposed to the theory, and post-rationalised success stories.

People devote much energy, time, and money to trying to show the ways communication programmes reach their targets, a relentless search for scientific proof of effectiveness, measurement nirvanas. Much less energy is spent measuring and analysing the all-too-human contributions to shaping destinies that occur in every meeting room, and every encounter – the brash, the frail, the elusive inputs that all have an effect.

2.   "Personally, I don't see it that way"

Here we look at what happens if you find yourself trapped in a myopic world. How do you orientate yourself when you can't see the wood from the trees, or those you are working with can't?

This collection of empirical examples shows what can happen when people won't hear things they don't want to hear.

3.   The Impact of Personal Perspectives

Brand Development

A brand is a territory, a state. Marks are made on it by those who cross it, protect it, build on it, fight over it, sell it, or destroy it. Users of brands are invited onto the turf as long as they pay a suitable amount for the right to enjoy whatever the reward that's offered by the brand's owner, for a period of time.

Here we explore in detail how personal agendas and perspectives have a much greater influence on brand trajectories and fortunes than most are willing to acknowledge.

Challenges to Objectivity – Numbers and Knowledge

There is much material on the subject of research, insights, experience and methodologies in marketing and communication environments. There are libraries of theses and papers on research approaches and ways of trying to craft messages to meet people's needs.

This huge business is also significantly influenced by factors that make objectivity a relative, not an absolute value, and we examine both the effect of this on working practice and what needs to be understood to manage the impact of this more effectively

New Product Development

The story continues with a close look at what is, for many, a future life-blood source for their enterprise, and what effect subjectivity can have both on products themselves, and on the communications strategies and executions they are then embedded in.

4.   Living in the Real World

People do not work in a bubble. Other influences, still driven by the impact of personality, are at work and shaping the creative environment in which ideas are created, presented and "sold." We look in this chapter at some of these influences and their impact.

Personal desire for both recognition and actual fame has grown exponentially over the last 50 years, and we examine its impact on the development of communications.

We also look at how the changing nature of communications themselves, together with rapid evolution in media opportunities and consumer awareness, have created a culture clash which traditional industry structures are still trying to come to terms with.

Culture, Behaviour and Expectation

In broadening our perspectives it is also important to look at the impact of societal culture on behaviour and expectation, and of course the obverse, through recent history. There are insights into how such often implicit or tacit workings in society have significantly influenced approaches and attitudes to communications codes and techniques. There is a special significance in the 'lag' effects these produce when dealing with brand definition, roles, and emerging expectations, together with communications types and functions.

The insight goes - needs remain constant, the ways of satisfying them change. We argue that needs change radically too. Challenging what brands are for, and challenging those who develop them, is a dangerous business, but a necessary one, because the conditions for and the nature of the worship of them have changed. There is still a large gap between brand management and users' expectations that is creating sustained dissonance and waste. Those who most recognise this are better equipped to help move brand 'gods' from their totemic face towards markets to a more integrated and balanced relationship between providers and users. This is a more fact and less faith-based approach to brand marketing and management.

We look at the ways brands are changing in the context of people's lives, and how those who manage them are often still locked in perspectives that are based in unwitting but outmoded views about authority and respect

5. Seeing the Light – Living with Diffraction

Improving perspective is vital for all communications. However straight and direct the beam we believe we are projecting with our messages, there will be a prism or lenses through which observers unwittingly fail to see what we are trying to say, and which will affect their reception and interpretation of it. We can only see this relatively, and this is tempered by our experience, which plays a role in how we construct our world view. This is an opportunity to look at how we get to approximations of truths, which do not exist in absolute terms, only relative ones.

6. Strategy. Are We Asking the Wrong Questions?

Strategy, or strategic thinking, can also be defined as perspective. A differentiating strategy needs discipline, knowledge, intelligence, inspiration, insight, and intuition. As perspective, strategy raises intriguing questions about intention and behaviour in a collective context, both by brand users, and by the companies that serve them. "In great companies, strategy becomes a cause, because strategy is about being different".[1]

In a less intellectually defined world, strategy, like other forms of innovation based on perceptual insights, needs to function beyond the constraints of job description boxes, or of departments, or of hierarchies, to support new creations, and new expressions. We suggest means of managing this from within existing boundaries and out into new territories that have worked in practice.

Before proposing what we believe the most relevant questions might be, we re-visit current common best practice, in the context of this question– are we simply asking the wrong questions?

7.   As a Client – Who Can I Turn to for the Best Advice?

Brands are described as being able, succinctly, to tell us what they are and what they stand for, especially those brands that hold leadership or iconic status. But are these values relevant for most brands these days? We still have some interesting challenges.

After we reach answers, who should control all this?

Many people in business want to be close to those who have the gift of bestowing rewards, and of showing that by taking a firm grasp of leading a team to deliver the wishes of the Bestower, they are also worthy followers, who will in turn become leaders and bestowers.

Here we see how perspective distorts clarity in understanding how leadership objectives and values are formed, and where they might take us to.

Part Two

Brands and Reality – How to Be Simply the Best

In the second part of the book, we look deeper at the ways in which brand users, as well as managers and owners, have shaped and been shaped by the historical context of their lives, and the impact this has had on brands and branding. We embrace this knowledge to move to a more contemporary perspective on the way things are, and might be. We look at brands in a refreshingly simple, pragmatic way. We go on to look at how structures, and the language we use to define people, processes and roles, might be modified to lead to the release of greater realistic value from brands and the organisations that manage them and work with them. We present a practical way of working to improve the ways in which marketing specialists can manage how better they can connect with users, and show how this delivers profitable results and more productive relationships.

8.   Stickiness and the Power of Simplification

We express our view that the need for and establishment of structures and belief systems within which to operate appears to be something almost hard-wired into our minds. Religion is a pervasive 'meme'. Brands, and the way we interact with them, are in many ways similar to this. There is little point in trying to reach an escape velocity from the very way our minds are structured, so what can we do to work more effectively with what we have already got? This is an adaptive approach.

9. A Simpler Way to Work with Brands More Effectively

Here we lay out a new classification for brands, and the ways in which this can be liberating for many brands that are being challenged because they don't appear to exemplify high emotional or star-quality status. It also opens the door to brand owners being able to realise value in new ways, and to release brands from dangerous burdens and assumptions that have become received wisdom in many operating environments. It is simple and practical. Too many tools are created that try to discover 'Holy Grail' brand opportunities through arcane and ultimately un-executable processes. It is time to move away from approaches that say you must try to give all brands some kind of higher ground. Many brands deliver perfectly acceptable levels of functionality, reliably, without users running away from an absence of emotional bonding. This should be the case for more brands, diverting them back to benefits without the need to over-invest in emotional chimaeras.

10. Predictable Barriers to Keeping It Simple

This chapter looks at ways people will object to change and find reasons to perpetuate the status quo. This is entirely normal, until people realise that what is presented is about positive change, and can lead to improvements on a number of levels, from the personal to the destiny of the brand being worked on.

11. Language and Structure – New Perspectives

Here we explore briefly some other controversial topics. Since language is about helping us both to structure our lives and classify things, we need to be more aware of its power in helping to construct and also create changes in the context of the ways we work, and the places we work in.

What we are called in the workplace, i.e. our job title, impacts on both our own and other people's views on how we operate. We argue here that current structures and titles are restrictive in today's communications environment, and our ability to create can be restricted by this. We need to think about working together in new ways to foster creativity.

12. Co-ignition – Getting More With Less

This is where we explain why we believe it is time for people to adopt a modestly different way of working based on a spectrum of real behaviour rather than filtered, overly diffracted or post-rationalised behaviour. We look at what this can be, why this is a good thing, how it works, and what it has already done for others. We call this managing risk and moving forwards, or, how safe exploration doesn't have to kill imagination.

13. Principles Driving this Approach

In this short chapter, we bring together the observations, points, and principles we have used to present our case, dispersed through the text and as key points at the ends of certain chapters.

14. What Goes Around...

A brief look and return full circle to the starting premise.

Influences & Sources

Part One

The Branded World and How I Made it So

1. It's More Subjective than You Might Think

There was a time when if you wanted to make yourself heard, and get yourself connected when you were away on business, you did this: You made a telephone call from your hotel room by picking up the heavy hand-set device that was connected by wire or cord to another base unit fixed to a wall, or that sat upon a table. You dialled a number that got you in touch with someone else in the hotel called an operator, usually a lady during the day, and a man during the night. She had the job of linking you to the person you wanted to speak to on another fixed telephone somewhere. The operator managed calls from several people by literally moving wires around a board to create new links. In this process she would often say, "Trying to connect you ..." in the hope that while she was filling time with this sign of action she would eventually produce a successful result.

That's how it was.

People living in those times would have thought – why would anyone want to carry a phone around with them? It's too big, and what would I do with all the wires? Today's technology will undoubtedly appear as cumbersome as this in twenty years, "Like, why did you have those keypads and things?"

That's how it will be.

These days if you want something done you iPhone it, or have someone you're paying to handle your iPhones do it. Or, you iPad it.

In the old days, people managed brands in ways that many would consider as primitive as the old fixed phones and their operating systems appear to be primitive today.

Whatever the technology, and the thinking about 'best practice', the drivers for change are the need to communicate, to be noticed, and often, the need to keep on the correct side of a quality/cost matrix. As human beings en masse we generally tend to lag behind the potential of new technology and ideas. We over-expect and then we underestimate the impact of things, and ideas. We make attempts to understand what's going on by containing experiences through definitions of use, regulation or legislation, which are then adapted as they are superseded by yet more new ideas and technologies.

What we want to introduce here is the basis for how to get more out of the ways brands can deliver value. This means understanding better what the drivers of brand user and brand owner behaviour are that lead to many of the shortfalls and disappointments in brand performance and expectations we see today, and what can be done to make some progress to closing these kinds of gaps and differences, profitably.

There is a need for a fresh perspective on what's really going on. This will unlock ways to make substantial improvements on brand investment value, returns, and brand destiny.

Take the example of the head office that issued its field service engineers with telephone-enabled Personal Digital Assistants. This was some time before Blackberries and iPhones, but only a few years, not decades ago. The original purpose was to enable those in the field to stay in touch with HQ, to order parts from stock, and to log jobs. What happened was that the service engineers themselves began to call other service engineers directly to help with problems they encountered but couldn't immediately handle on their own. This led to a sharing of experience and a collective raising-up of knowledge levels. It also improved productivity and morale in ways the centre never envisaged, since it bypassed them. It was a new way of connecting, and being productively connected. It constituted a significant change in perception and perspective.

It enhanced the company's overall performance, goodwill, and reputation.

Or take the man struggling to find ways to access data that was held in a widely distributed network on different formats. The answer Tim Berners-Lee developed spawned the Internet as we know it. He was simply looking for a better way to connect. Then along came other forms of social networking.

Our approach breaks down some of the myths or received wisdom about brands and management, innovation skills and ownership, and presents practical ways of reconfiguring resources to get better ways to connect and create value between brands, their owners and managers, and their users. This does not mean that one form of branded pickled onions should be a Facebook friend, or its equivalent.

We observe a number of retrospective analyses on why 'conventional wisdom' about marketing communications is of decreasing relevance. But there are few attempts to suggest alternative modes of operation, other than the universal uptake of new media formats. Here we offer a point of view on how to move things forward in a tangible and practical way.

It has been said that brands are the sum of the information people carry around in their heads about them. This information is put into a context bounded by an individual's general views on the world. Brand owners spend a great part of their time trying to build bridges between what they consider to be the holistic role of their brands, and these individual worlds. That's the theory.

In practice, brands are also very much a function of the highly subjective influence of the individuals and teams who are or who are allegedly responsible for them, and their destinies can be intertwined.

Much energy, time, and money is devoted to demonstrating the ways these bridge-building endeavours operate, how communication programmes have reached their targets, and what comprises the relentless search for scientific proof of effectiveness, measurement nirvanas. Much less energy is spent measuring and analysing the all too human contributions to shaping destinies that occur in every meeting room, and in every encounter – the brash, the frail, the quixotic, the elusive inputs, which are often more critical.

Maybe because there's not enough time, or because all undesirable and difficult-to-measure activities are conveniently written off as 'politics', very real effects that influence brand development are not captured, and lessons are not learned. Potential contributions can be filtered out because, "they're from department X, and have no right to comment on that". Businesses and brands are being constantly shaped by unrecorded events that have a huge significance on destinies – or simply on the 'background radiation' of brand lives. Dilbert went some way to capture these kinds of behaviours, but they are rarely traced in hard-nosed summaries of marketplace results and brand-building histories. They become the anecdotes of retired successful CEOs. Otherwise they are momentary slices in the office day, simply put down as the way of the world. It's the way it is.

But these human factors won't go away. Many folks are happy to divert attention to research methodologies or formulae, or ascribe success to belief-systems in the hope of discounting the variable contributions of real peoples' subjectivity to a desired business model and set of goals. They are only achieving pyrrhic victories. The processes used to justify consequential decisions and actions are often themselves key inhibitors to the development of fresh forms of constructive and innovative thinking, expression, and evaluation.

In many walks of life, there is a growing body of literature about how conflicts have been decided by caprices, in nature or through human intervention – called the 'Hinge Factor' in military terms, or Black Swans,[1] – an approach that has popularised David Hume's problem of induction. These sets of observations acknowledge the role of chance, of mistakes, of poor decisions. They are rooted in reality. But in marketing, dreams about a world where Sinclair C5s and New Coke would go on to world domination are only ridiculed posthumously. In too many of today's marketing environments there's apparently little room for human error, whatever the statements about managing risk say, so the pursuit of disciplined, scientific rigour is the name of the game, even if the reality is different. If only scientists themselves had pursued this it might have produced different results, but the subjective views and egos of scientists and their pet theories has influenced the path of scientific knowledge and breakthroughs through most of time, and that's before we let things like the influence of Religion or War or both into the scenario. We hope that marketing can develop at a different pace than the cynical observation about science which once said: science progresses through funerals. Successful marketing can enjoy incremental victories by learning to recognise and then manage these human elements better, as opposed to either being in denial about them, or by trying to kill them off.

So before all the brand histories and effectiveness papers are cleansed of these awkward subjectivities, let's capture just some of the ways in which the brands we buy are shaped. Since we will be dealing with a spread of types of experience here, some of which people would describe as failures, a number of the actual businesses and players have been protected, without the point of the stories being diluted. In any case, should you happen to have been close to the events, you'll know who you are.

And what's the point? Is there any evidence to suggest that people learn from the past, from other people's mistakes, and apply these lessons? There is evidence. We want to help the evidence reach a wider audience.

Whatever has been done has counted in some way, good or bad. What also counts is what we elect to do right at this moment, now, and if these observations help you enjoy the moment of being accountable a little more, with a higher chance of realising results on the positive part of the performance curve, then the encounters will have been worthwhile.

> **There is a need for a fresh perspective on what's really going on. This will unlock ways to make substantial improvements on brand investment value, returns, and brand destiny.**

2. "Personally, I don't see it that way"

One of the first observations is that things are almost never the way they seem. Often they are not nearly as straightforward as they initially look. We exemplify this by looking at some situations in marketing and communications, from differing perspectives.

Perspective One. What constitutes truth?

"The truth, the whole truth, and everything but the truth ..."

The first time the communications agency person thought she was being objective about a new product development produced an interesting result. Between returning from the client company and entering home base, a phone call had been made to say she wouldn't be needed on the business any more.

"What did you say?" asked the manager who had fielded the call. She replayed the meeting in a faithful way, from her perspective, and the boss said, "Ah, now I understand." He called back the client and she was re-installed. She was about to learn her first lesson about impartiality.

In this case, the client company was desperate to extend its product portfolio into new areas, and new revenue streams, or so the script went. This was envisaged to create a huge impact on the company's future, and secure the hopefully positive legacy of the soon-to-be-retired Senior Vice President who believed this. Nothing would stop a new product launch, its inevitable triumph, and its associated accolades. The product was a new over-the-counter medicine. It would sweep away the incumbents.

Targeted users would beat a path to this new product's doorway to relief.

Except that the product was aimed at acute sufferers of an ailment, who were often old, and frequently financially constrained. They had become well entrenched in the habit of using the tried and tested brand leader, almost as a placebo. They would chew these, a dime a dozen, like sweets. They had an armoury of tales about why they suffered from their debilitating ailment, and why nothing would ever really cure it – something like changing dietary habits was at least a decade away from consideration. The ailment was a fact of life for these people. So a product that came with as few as twenty tablets a pack, at a price four times that of the brand leader with its fifty or hundred tablets a pack, and with a complex story of efficacy to tell, was going to sweep the board? That's what the representative asked. Naïve or what?

What should she have said? Ah, that's truly revolutionary, a real breakthrough, and we'll have the old folks eating out of our hands in no time?

You'll get different answers according to who you ask. And that's the point. Who do you ask?

But in fact the first question should be "What do you expect to hear?" So many people have been conditioned to respond only as an echo to a client's projected success it's hardly surprising there is cynicism about the chances of obtaining objective counsel from the likes of communication consultants geared only to securing easy forms of revenue. In this world, communications agencies are compensated for cure not prevention, for creating solutions, not for recommending doing nothing, or abandoning a lost cause. And sometimes, even if the agency has the courage to try to deliver objective advice, it doesn't always go down well.

Imagine an account manager faced with a new senior client, whose first request is "I don't want agency flannel, I want you to tell me what you really think". So the account manager does just that, not rudely, but very politely, saying that the very famous old fast moving consumer goods brand being discussed needed to be made relevant to contemporary life.

The client says nothing to disagree with this in the meeting, but the next day, the agency Managing Director is summoned to a meeting where he is asked to remove the account manager, because the client doesn't like his attitude. Fortunately, the account person in question had another client who valued his intelligence and objectivity, so he didn't lose his job, but it's just another example of how the human factor impacts on everyday decisions. That may just be life, but it has profound effects on business and personal fortunes.

We once had a situation where smart middle managers from Procter & Gamble were hired in to a then rather traditional brewing business. After a few months the new boys said a particular product should be reformulated and advertised as a 'new, improved' taste experience. This was rapidly and haughtily dismissed by the incumbent senior management who pronounced that such a thing could never be done because it suggested the previous product wasn't the finest it could have been. Business stagnated for years.

It's only human to try to avoid bringing bad news to masters with big sticks, unless you genuinely think you are being helpful in the first place. Is there any way out of the shoot the messenger syndrome? As Clint Eastwood once pointed out to a trigger-happy challenger in one of his master of understanding weakness roles – "Dying ain't no way of making a living, boy". So we'll have to look elsewhere for answers.

Turning to the learning of some of the world's Intelligence communities, they would say that facts about an enemy's capabilities don't constitute actionable intelligence until you also understand what your enemy's intentions are. It was easy to assess what the first company's ability to produce new tablets was. What the account person didn't appreciate was the client's desire to go to a new market for themselves under any contrived circumstances, including ignoring unwelcome test market evidence that clearly revealed the huge obstacles to succeeding with this product in the core user group that the agency representative had also figured. The real driver of the agenda in this scenario was the wish to extend the company's portfolio into new areas, and a lasting legacy for the soon to be retiring brand champion. A little shortfall in appropriate user responses wasn't going to taint the objective.

Had the hapless account person uncovered this insight from her own boss before the client encounter, her line of commentary and questioning may have been different: "Do you have any clinical evidence we can use to help support the case for the price premium that would help us with the communications brief?" Or she may have understood this person's position more clearly if she had had a deeper insight into the desires of the corporate strategists. Managing the relationship for the longer term may have been easier if she'd had the wider perspective going in.

What happened?

The target group had short-term curiosity, deep pockets, and very short arms. The new product launch did not enjoy a long life. It was an interesting lesson in why some brands come to market – really. It would never have figured in a case study.

Here are some other behavioural insights.

There was a communications company that decided to move out of a capital city to be nearer its predominantly green-field clients and demonstrate its commitment to being on hand to service their needs. They promptly lost much of their business. They hadn't worked out that many of their clients chose them because they were in the capital, and because it gave them an excuse to be out of the office occasionally and having a good time.

One corporate treasurer's only concern when dealing with an investment bank was, "Will I still get an invitation to the bank's box for the finals of the US Tennis Open if a junior salesperson covers my business?"

Robert Citron, the treasurer of Orange County, California, managed to have his name attached to the loss of more than $1.5 billion through derivative trading on the behalf of his unknowing flock. He was sure there was no risk when things were going well. "I am one of the largest investors in America. I know these things." This was back in July 1993. On December 6th 1994 Orange County filed for bankruptcy. The court proceedings unveiled Citron's investment strategy. He relied on the advice of a psychic and a mail order astrologer for financial guidance, using a $4.50 chart prepared by an Indianapolis star-reader to help manage Orange County's money.

Country leaders have also been prone to using such guidance. The learning is that there are always plenty of people around who want to be led to fortune and then fall into its downside, disaster. This is apparent from a social pathology: psychopaths rally followers.

The world of brands has its own share of weird and wonderful characters alike.

Perspective Two. The trouble with myopia

What happens when you find yourself trapped in a myopic world? How do you orientate yourself when you can't see the wood from the trees, or those you are working with can't? When people's minds and imaginations are locked onto their brand so tightly that they can only be short-term masters of self-defence in a besieged world, it can be very difficult to prise them off their supporting rocks or out of their castle keeps. It's hard to get them to see there's still a land or an ocean out there that may contain other ways of surviving, prospering, carrying messages, or attracting new and curious prospects.

What do you say to the marketing director who looked at a still picture of custard being poured onto a sponge pudding and said, "I don't like the sponge. It denigrates the value of the custard".

"Mmm, that sounds just like what a typical user would say, I guess you're right."

And from the same company, where there was the case of a new form of an old, liked, familiar dessert. This time around it appeared in little pots, ready-made, looking not unlike yoghurts. Convenient? You bet. Housewives looking for treats for their kids wouldn't have to mess around with powders and milk and time-consuming messy combinations. Just reach for a pot, open it, give Johnny a spoon, and watch the ensuing delight. This sounded like real progress. But wait a second. The product in this form didn't taste as good as the original. It came in pots that looked like yoghurt pots – so where would you put them? In the fridge of course. And what happened then? They de-structured because they were ambient products. Just how many things can be thrown away in the search for more convenient forms of delivery?

Needless to say, in the company's drive to reduce its powder technology dependence while creating a form that users would still entertain to keep consuming their products, marketing people connected to these kinds of projects just got promoted onwards and upwards. We all know that around 80% of new product launches fail, so if everyone who ever came up with a bummer was fired, there'd be few left to take the credit for successes. Anyway, don't we say that failures are just experience, or are they managed risk-taking? It depends on the operating culture you find yourself in.

In another place at another time, the meeting appeared to have gone well, with ten out of eleven clients agreeing with the proposed wardrobe selections for a commercial being developed for Spain. At this point the Belgian marketing man, who was on a posting in Spain, pronounced that he couldn't accept the recommendation that the principal actress in the commercial was going to wear a blue blouse. Why might that be, asked the agency representative tentatively? "Because blue is the colour of fascism and Spanish women will have negative associations with it". You can't make up these kinds of reactions. They rarely make it into official Brand History Books.

We come to the December pre-production meeting for a

commercial for a plastic-bottled cleaning product, to run across six or seven European markets. After thirty minutes the co-ordinating client called a time-out as no client company participants could agree on anything. After a further two hours a form of consensus was being reached when some-one chirped up that nothing could be finalised because Turkey wasn't in the meeting. The commercials director, somewhat tired by this stage, said "But it just wouldn't be Christmas without Turkey, would it?" After another hour, and a long discussion about plastic bottles and labels and sign-off lines, a form of wrap-up had been agreed. "Anything else?" we asked. At this point the relatively junior and previously unspoken Austrian client produced a large cardboard box from under the table and said, "This is our pack in Austria".

In another case we witness an example of marketing people who think they are so close to the user that they have a sure fire success on their hands. In user observation, which we will return to later, dedicated brand managers witness housewives adding additional ingredients, such as tomatoes, to dry (dehydrated) packet sauce mixes – so conclude that there is a major opportunity for a "more-tomato-y" variant. Research and Development oblige, and no one questions anything until the communications brief arrives in the agency and someone points out the brief which says "no comparison with original recipe". The client responds by saying that they don't want any cannibalisation, so the creative process begins. It's only when pre-test results come in that common sense prevails. Users can't understand what the difference is between the original and line extension, and anyway don't want a line extension. They put tomatoes in mixes because it makes them feel more involved in the cooking process, and therefore less fussed about using a short-cut.

In these illustrations we witness pieces of thinking about a brand that were so far removed from the likely user response as to be wholly useless, even in the most directive of qualitative research groups looking to uncover negative associations in communications proposals. Then we see the classic, "But it's different in my market" reaction. In another we see the sublimation of proven user values like taste and goodness to unwanted extra convenience in the form of a weakened product. Full marks awarded for trying some innovation with long-established brands, but fewer for turning a blind eye to data and experience that didn't support the desired new direction at all.

31

The lesson is that just because you start to drive enough times the long way around the mountain and not over it doesn't mean the mountain goes away.

Perspective Three. More surprises

"Getting to know you…"

It was time for a much-travelled, long standing and important client to move on to a new assignment. He had to be sent off with a truly memorable memento. One of the team knew he had a particular interest, so a graduate trainee was sent off on a search for a genuine South American Indian machete to add to the client's already impressive collection, in London. After three days of looking, calling, visiting, and negotiating with the none-too-common sources of such items in the city, the answer came back that such a thing could be acquired, but at a very interesting price. "Gee, buy the guy a goddamn globe," came the response. The leaving party was a success.

Then it was the turn of the client service person to say good-bye to a tough client as he moved on to a new job himself. He knew the last project with this client had been really difficult, and he was leaving at a critical time, before its completion, with some relief. "I sure am glad I won't be around when the shit hits the fan on this one," he quipped in his leaving remarks.

The client immediately piped up "Buddy, you *are* the fan".

The marketing director of a financial services business was also moving on to pastures new. As the farewell lunch moved on beyond dessert, the supplier asked if he had any advice to pass on to the team, "Yes, he said. Don't work in the financial service business." This may have been driven by the fact that the agency had developed a campaign that the client supported, only to have it killed by a qualitative researcher whose worldview indicated it would not work. The brand users' actual points of view were never presented, nor faithfully represented, in the research debrief. The client put his faith in the researcher, and the promised solution never went further. The researcher claimed objectivity and a desire "only to help".

And on another tough day in the office, a distressed art director didn't want to hear his work had been rejected again. The account handler thought it would be a good idea to try and smooth over the situation, and knowing the art director would by now have taken refuge in a nearby bar with his friends, went to offer an olive-branch.

"Can I buy you a drink?"

"I'll never be that thirsty," came the reply.

They went on to become good friends. Oh, and the work got better, sales were good, awards were awarded, and everyone lived happily ever after, well, at least until the next brief came through. And funnily enough, none of this made it into the story of how the campaign came to be developed, and the brand enjoyed further success, which of course was a decorative canvas of strategic insights and econometric analyses, as far as the brand's official case study had it. But if that relationship hadn't developed, the brand's destiny might well have been quite different.

Before we move on to look at brands themselves, consider a little experiment. On one side of your desk or screen, assemble a list of the books and cases and communication effectiveness papers that you've read or been referred to or seen précis of in magazines and newspapers and downloads. They're all the ones that tell you about how things moved from good to great, or other variations of excellence. Now, on the other side, assemble a kind of family tree of people you know, or knew, who were involved in brands you work or worked on. Capture the names of the ones who fought hard to push through a position or direction against the grain. Remember the ones who blocked every move. Recall the ones who supported your view, and the ones who didn't. For every brand there will be an unrecorded trace map. Think how things might have been different if you change the names around.

Now remember a great experience you had, a holiday or a hotel stay. Apart from the fabulous location, try and think about something that really made a difference for you. Often it's about an individual who made a moment magical, like a great cocktail barman, a helpful concierge, a supportive maître d', an engaging guide, a chance encounter. The people matter. You know this already. What we need to get better at is recognising and harnessing the good from the bad in all this.

We will talk about methods and methodologies, but we will also talk about the manner of things. It's obviously people as much as processes that truly make things happen, but the perceptions and the influences of all those who truly affect brand destinies are not sufficiently factored in when we look at the commonplace histories and case studies of marketing successes and failures.

Charles Channon spoke about this way back in the 80s in his piece on *Agency Thinking and Agencies as Brands*, noting that while different agencies approach the creation of campaigns in different ways, these differences are usually instinctive and merely reflect the personalities of top management.

Another agency watcher commented on the famous Saatchi brothers that Charles Saatchi had no interest in philosophising or intellectualising about advertisements, and that to the brothers advertising was either "terrific or shit".

Then there was the creative director who used a 'Sooty' bear glove puppet to pronounce to teams showing new ideas that "Sooty thinks they're crap."

The legendary coupling of client Anthony Simmonds-Gooding and agency man Frank Lowe was the absolute diamond that brought the shine to Heineken.

We aim to demonstrate that the improved management of the perspectives people bring into the creation of brand destinies can lead to the creation of greater levels of brand performance than the current marketing models suggest.

---

3. The Impact of Personal Perspectives

Brand Development

Let's just open a couple of pages of one very old Brand Family Album.

Some people make a living out of building them. Some make a living out of out of owning them, or selling them. Some live out their lives measuring them every which way. Before we look further at ways of describing brands, let's just glimpse at what some of the measurement makers and takers have classified as brands over the last generation or so.

Britain's top grocery brands in the ancient time of 1989 were:

Persil	PG Tips
Coca-Cola	Beans
Flora	Whiskas
Chum	Arielx
Nescafe	

So imagine a typical dream marketer's day, as we turn the old album's pages. We see mums in neighbouring houses compete to wash their family's clothes better, so ensuring their kids will have a brighter future. They take a break with quality tea or coffee, go to the super clean and germ-free lavatory with its soft seductive toilet tissue, feed the dog/cat to keep them alive longer and fitter, give their kids the best branded beans on toast spread with new and healthy Flora, and a Coke to wash it down, preparing for the moment their husband walks in with the next household financial contribution. In the background Burt Bacharach and Hal David's song plays quietly on the family stereo - *Wives and Lovers*. It's a perfectly balanced world of consumption and staying ahead of the Jones's. Let's put that in the context of a few newspaper headlines in the world at the same time:

- *Berlin Wall Falls*

- *Tiananmen Square Crackdown*

- *A Beeper that makes Headlines – new pager offers text displays*

- *DJ Jazzy Jeff and The Fresh Prince release their gold-selling 3rd album.*

What kind of world were these marketing people living in? How quickly do perspectives change?

Look at it another way. One year later The Interbrand Company in 1990 stated, "Based upon our evaluation, the world's top ten brands are, in rank order, Coca-Cola, Kellogg's, McDonald's, Kodak, Marlboro, IBM, American Express, Sony, Mercedes-Benz, and Nescafe."

Financial World[1] magazine published its list of top valued brands in 1993, including Marlboro, Coca-Cola, and Intel.

Has anything much changed today?

Millward Brown's *Brandz* report recorded their 2007 top ten as:

Google	GE (General Electric)
Microsoft	Coca Cola
China Mobile	Marlboro
Wal Mart	Citigroup
IBM	Toyota

And for some more headlines just choose your preferred search engine and download these kinds of surveys live now.

The compilers and the criteria for evaluation are as varied as the ultimate values ascribed. All are searching for a combination of tangible and intangible properties that constitute their definition of a brand. Few venture to try and predict a list of either brands or values for ten years from now, so they are not positioning themselves as leaders in the futurology business. Whatever time you take to siphon through this kind of material, there's always a consensus that building brands is harder than it's ever been, and for those who get it right, the rewards are also bigger than they've ever been, at least for a while.

The conclusion most of these measurers and compilers reach goes something like this: Brands can therefore acquire considerable value. The value is shared, apparently, between owners, users, and any intermediaries who can legitimise a case for involvement. One of the key questions then must be whether brands can only be brands if they can show continued accumulated growth, or the ability to be given renewed leases of life. What then do we call a declining brand? A senior brand?

Let's just throw in another perspective, simply because there's a debate coursing particularly in academic circles, and it might extend the discussion. It's about the way ideas get into our heads, and others. We'll be looking more closely at this later.

What brands constitute today is twofold. At one level they are a form of memes[3], concepts modified by those who come into contact with them, and whose subsequent interaction with others modifies them in turn again. They are also very often the gewgaws of their owners, whatever protestations of user empowerment and brand management are out there.

Some of the world's famous historical figures can be characterised or categorised as acquisitors[4], those who used religion, politics and their understanding of human psychology, or what we incorrectly describe as animal behaviour, basically to get and keep what they wanted. Not surprisingly, that usually meant some form of meaningful wealth to them - gold, land, wives, husbands, fame, and reputation.

Brands are one of the new-ish toys through which grand acquisitors fulfil their needs for fame and fortune. Many brands show resilience powerful enough to survive the short-term attentions of a number of people who have close encounters with them in the early stages of their careers, and sometimes even to outwit those who try and control the big picture at the tops of their also often branded companies. The kinds of daily interactions that take place between owners and managers are usually not available to scrutiny outside the companies where they take place. They are buried in the normal systems of operations that support a brand's life, like cell regeneration and replacement. But every so often someone comes along and gives us the benefit of their hindsight about what was going on. Look at Donald Keogh from Coca-Cola, or Lou Gerstner who turned around IBM. Whatever their tradecraft marketing and investment skills, they always point to major human factors as the reasons things hadn't happened or changed and that had placed the companies in weakened positions – attitudes, blind faith, misperceptions

A brand is like a territory, a state. Marks are made on it by those who cross it, protect it, build on it, fight over it, sell it, or destroy it. So-called users of brands are invited onto the turf as long as they pay a suitable amount for the right to enjoy the rewards offered by the brand's owner for a period of time. Other than that people often pay only a passing role in the brand's destiny at the hands of the acquisitors. It is idealistic to believe that brand users have majority control over brand destiny in a large number of cases. They can cause plenty of consternation, like with Perrier, Coca-Cola, Toyota, and so on. But plenty of brands and corporations with brand values have been damaged or worse by their owners and managers, leaving users and employees in the shadows. Enron, WorldCom, Parmalat, Arthur Andersen, Lehman Bros, Swissair, and others, come to mind.

Don't be fooled into thinking the use of phrases like 'customer-driven' and 'customer-centric' are often anything other than politically correct ways of buying time to get on with the real business at hand, which is driven for many by altogether different motives. And anyway, it should be easier to sympathise with those who say the user has never really been able to tell people what they want next until someone puts it in front of them. As the oft-quoted Henry Ford noted, if you'd asked people what they wanted, to get from a - b quicker, they'd have demanded a faster horse. The customer comes eighth. Then they're allowed to say they don't like something. That's called choice. This is still the case.

The Japanese got on fine without the wheel for centuries after the rest of us were rolling along. Now they find they can't live without cars, and it's just as taxing living with them. Wal-Mart gave customers what they want, yet often it was allegedly at the expense of showing any respect for their own employees' contributions to their acknowledged success. And how many qualitative research reports did you ever read that said "Hey, if you can give me a 170gram GPRS mobile phone, blue-tooth enabled, with camera and high-speed download capabilities, that would be really cool", in 1985? Wanting and giving don't always dovetail.

Take a survey of innovations twenty years ago. Technology was supposed to revolutionise the arts by making them omnipresent. The role of the radio, its later enabling transistor, TV, video cassette players – all were catalogued as transformers of perception, yet there is no mention of the mobile phone, DVD players, or the Internet. How could there be? Even though they were around, there had yet to be a true explosion of uptake – it was, after all, only 1994.[4]

Brands may be many things, and they are certainly the result of behaviour practised on their behalf by those whose time is ascribed to them as part of their career. As we have noted, much of this behaviour is unrecorded, not captured. It can take brands in very different directions. It can support enormous, prolonged myths. It can respond to received wisdom. It can make them, and their managers, highly resistant to necessary forms of iconoclasm. It can furnish wardrobes of emperor's new clothes. It can swear allegiance to fictions that drown common sense. Even in small ways, the influence of those charged with managing brands on a day-to-day basis is significant, and not in ways they would themselves often suggest.

Take these examples.

There was a client whose advertising agency regarded him as being very conservative. When faced with an advertising idea whose initial manifestation was a commercial which featured tiny babies swimming underwater, no one on the team expected anything other than a "no". The client asked for 24 hours to think about it, and called the next day to say "Go ahead. No research. Just make the film." What made the difference? His wife, who saw the idea and liked it. She was eight months pregnant.

Another client rejected a proposal for a poster to celebrate a forthcoming royal baby. It was rejected in case there was anything wrong with the baby on arrival. The client was very sensitive about babies (rightly so), but the fact that she couldn't have children made her even more acutely so.

What about the man who, having approved a script to be produced, took one look at the first edit of the commercial, walked out of the room silently and disappeared? He called later that evening. "I'm sorry," he said. "But last night my sixteen year old daughter turned up at the house with her new boyfriend, who looked exactly like the person you cast in the commercial, and I just couldn't handle it." He put this down to the first time there'd ever been a crossover between work and home for him, and he then approved the commercial – saving everyone a considerable amount of time and money. But it could easily have been different.

Or the man who appeared to approve or reject work on no rational basis – until it was discovered that he usually turned down work when something very important was happening to him – he was a diabetic, and the need for insulin affected his response to creative work. Understanding this led to an improvement in managing the relationship, and a better overall output to the work supporting the brand, and its fortunes.

Sometimes personal agendas can prove very costly. In one case a client had had a concept for a new product and then left the company before it was truly brought to life. Circumstances led to his return to the fold after the product had become a brand and had been successfully launched through another team. He then dedicated himself to trying to kill all presentations of the product that didn't harmonise with his original conception, which did significant damage to the new brand's chances of a long and prosperous life. Is this right? Again, outcomes often depend on the brand owner's operating culture. At Coca-Cola for instance, the new Chief Executive Officer[5] discovered that the operating culture was strangling the brand, and its managers were aggressively holding on to traditions about the brand that were no longer relevant to the market. This was a great example of the Halo Effect[6] dominating the reality of the market.

For over fifty years, a major detergent brand capitalised on what was considered to be a profitable and mutually dependent relationship – the brand and its key user, the mother. This is a brand that, for almost all its life, had been run by middle-class men, whose wives often stayed at home to help run the family. This guaranteed that for decades there was no fundamental change in the attitude of management to the way the brand talked to its key user group. This led to a progressive loss of strength in terms of a relevant user relationship, except in the heads of the brand custodians for whom this brand was a badge of excellence in terms of their subsequent performance and status within the organisation, once again, in their heads.

These human factors are deeply significant in the way brand trajectories are formed, yet their role is rarely noted in detail. What exists is a huge gap between what is supposed to have worked, and the real dynamics of what goes on. We are looking at the effects of this from a number of perspectives. We also talk about ways to move on and forward from the lag effects that these approaches to managing brands engender. If the ability to identify highly subjective perspectives and manage them diminishes, either through lack of experience or the quality of relationships with people, the fortunes of service enterprises and brands themselves will be hostages to more highly narrowcast or biased perspectives. These kill brands.

It is an interesting gap. For instance, in a John Grisham book, you rarely find much in the way of theses about business models. And in most business books, outside of publications like those from the Harvard Business Review, you are rarely entertained to a re-play of meetings and dialogues as part of the action creating the case to be analysed. Each approach fits its genre. It is this form of expectation and preconditioning which perpetuates the gap. Yet it is in the gaps that the source of much of the fundamental behaviour that is consequent to a brand's fortunes occurs. Why is that?

Marketing having raised claim to being a professional discipline over the last forty years finds it messy and unpalatable to have to come to terms with the extant, elementary and unchanged behaviour of individuals and groups in organisations. Corporate codes of behaviour disguise the raw values that still drive people to want more power, control, money, and respect, to differing degrees according to the individual and organisation cultures in question.

Let's look briefly again at the human factor in that most objective of tools and approaches to getting it right in brand building – market research. We'll be returning to this subject again in more depth, but for an introduction, let's welcome you to what we call the Demeter Moment.

Many clients become sporadically bored with familiar research tools, so there are often opportunities for those with new solutions to bring a little light into the tired eyes of brand managements looking to leverage a part of their portfolio towards new levels of share and profitability. This is of course sometimes matched with their personal 'brand equity' development, formally labelled ambition.

A six-day workshop is established, where thirty carefully chosen candidates are invited to re-invent and position their brands based on Greek mythology. Charles Handy did this for organisations years ago in his study *The Gods of Management*[7] but not everybody knows that. Why do this?

Because the Greek Gods, wait for this, represent the same elemental power that resides in brands. Ergo, who is sadly not a god, leaves Demeter as the obvious archetype for a detergent brand, yes, a detergent brand, because it's all about caring and motherhood. Well, at least that's what all the senior male clients believed. The women thought differently, and were only saved by a brave outsider who said "Doing the laundry is on a par with putting out the milk bottles in terms of demonstrating care for the family", an analogy that only makes sense in parts of England of course, where in some places fresh milk can still be delivered daily to the front door of your house, and you leave the empties out at night for collection the next morning, and so on.

You can imagine, for it is not recorded except in the memory of the person who recounted this experience, the collective raising of male eyebrows, the slow collusive nodding of heads, and the little smiles that mimed, "There, there, she just doesn't understand the brand."

It was Raymond Chandler[8] who said "Playing chess is the most wasteful use of intelligence I've ever seen outside of an advertising agency." But it's spreading out. The ability of people to create brand metaphors that cannot subsequently be turned into communication materials for prospects and users is very high.

It goes something like this, only it takes a lot longer to get there. "If Brand X were a car, it would be a European family saloon; if it was a flower it would be a tulip; if it was a philosopher it would be Wittgenstein – now go write some of those communications."

Fortunately for the kinds of research companies that choose to practise these kinds of approaches, there are still plenty of people about who are looking for the next conceptual mousetrap, so the business and its variations go profitably on.

If brands are big boys' toys, and very occasionally girls', what happens in the playground? The big boys say "It's my ball so I'm the captain", and the little boys, those who want to play, play at idolizing the big boys until the day they get the ball, or one like it, themselves. While they're waiting they are crusaders, warriors, courtiers, brand terrorists, statesmen.

The badge they wear says, "My brand is the most important thing in the world". The message is, look at how I serve this, and so you.

Take a UK high-street clearing bank, although ubiquity is a stretched notion these days. All these banks are seen as being almost interchangeable by users, at a basic level. There's still an 'us and them' factor in this relationship, reinforced by behaviour over many years. The response to trying to close this gap between the banks' services and its customers stated needs, in one particular case, was to go to market with the message "We're Big". This probably made the CEO feel his compensation package was therefore publicly justified, but did nothing for a customer base that feels that's precisely the problem when it comes to getting something they want. Everyone in the boardroom says "We're big, let's be open about it and tell the world. We're the best."

It is actions like this that give breaks to number two operators and challenger brands. But it's easy to see why people are seduced by these approaches – in organisations. Leading from the front is what old-style warriors often did. It's a proven formula, and it often works if you have lots of armed supporters either side of you. Can you lead from behind?

In so-called democratic organisational climates there are people who will say, "I will launch this brand worldwide, and it will be different". They believe that this display will drive a mandate forward. In those very same organisations there is equal and opposite energy applied to stopping just that, often based on entirely personal reasons, or grudges.

Take a multi-national client who wanted to harmonise a group of local brands into one common positioning globally – not one common creative execution, please note – just one common positioning. He invested in research in all his key markets, and if looked at objectively, this research suggested that all the brands in question could occupy common territory across a diverse range of markets. But no one, apart from the global leaders, wanted to look at the research objectively – and that included key players in the communication agencies. So enormous amounts of time, money and energy were expended on proving why the global recommendation – for a common positioning, remember – "will not work in my region". This had nothing to do with objectivity, and everything to do with personal agendas in that particular organisation and its specific structure and culture. Only when the CEO and the Board stated their Company strategy was to seek efficient synergies of precisely this type, and compensation was aligned to the goal, did people change their behaviour. There was nothing wrong with the brand harmonising program per se. It was a contextual problem based on previous behaviour and 'norms'.

The new business director of one agency, looking at start-ups as potentially new clients, was told to forget pursuing two of these because in the first instance the managing director had a monthly lunch with a senior director of an established company in the same field, and that would lead to a bigger win for the agency, notwithstanding the strong likelihood that this would never happen at all, and the protracted regular lunches were just that. His contact was at ICL, a company most people have forgotten about. The prospect was called Apple Computers. In the second instance, hanging on to a poor quality vodka brand for short term returns meant telling the Swedish upstarts from Absolut that their little launch plans had no future or proper credentials.

Then there was the data that indicated there was an opportunity for regional beer brands to get established again in the UK. The presentation to the agency management team was dismissed as piffle, because they were blinded by the revenue stream from their national lager and beer brand accounts. Guess what happened?

You may have witnessed one or several projects being killed off because your boss doesn't like the person down the corridor who just had a bright idea. We will look at how this can be countered without getting caught up in the cross-fire.

Brands with worldwide potential are held back because of personal resistance to the project leader, and the project. Resistance comes through the simple declaration of disbelief in the expensive research assembled. How do you feel? It depends.

Some brand managers really are terrorists. They are fanatics and fundamentalists, armed with brand-defending tools and a total faith in toothpaste, or cat-food, demanded of them by the culture of their organisations. Would you resist them? It depends. But this isn't natural behaviour is it? It's learned. It's acquired.

When one of the sources of examples in this book first entered a media organisation as a graduate, it was with the naïve belief that being there had something to do with assimilating the way things were done quickly, and then developing those in innovative and profitable ways. It was genuinely thought the hiring was for the ability to think and see things in a different light. It was then alarming to discover no-one was meant to have any such thing as an original idea or approach for at least two years, until one had effectively been institutionalised. This was to ensure everyone would represent the ways of the company to the world at large, a process that held up precisely what their philosophy claimed they did best for others, that is, develop ideas that would change things.

"Would you care to elaborate on what you mean when you say you want fresh thinkers?" was probably not going to be a job-securing interview question. Even at that stage there were qualifiers at work.

Then there was the time one of us was asked to present a paper at a media conference whose audience included a good section of twenty-five to thirty year old managers in toiletries and cosmetics companies. Thinking they would be already versed in the details of a particular brand's well-publicised success, we thought we'd use the platform to present some thoughts about product portfolio management, which had been cleared with the conference organisers. The result was a total non-response from the delegates. These people just wanted charts and checklists. They were all wearing the same kind of two-piece power-suit of the moment, and they all had the same attitude. It was one of the few environments then where there was only a minority of men to be seen. Now, were all these women fundamentally the same when they were at university five or so years before? After all, they were all brand-folks now. What had happened on the way? Somehow they'd all subscribed to their own projection of the uber-manager, and were now vigorously paying their dues, fearsomely supporting the brands they were developing. Almost none of them had retained any concept of reality in terms of the references they used to talk about the brands they were managing; even if they were normal in all other aspects of the ways they conducted their lives.

How can a tired old brand with no product improvements be repackaged and expected to sell to an audience who already feel it is something out of touch with their needs, under a positioning describing it as a 'vertical bath experience'? How can a toothpaste company say the taste of its products has no effect on user buying behaviour? How can a coffee producer tell you that although in blind taste tests users always preferred the competition, consumers were actually wrong because "our product uses the best beans"? And these issues shouldn't be avoided by throwing down the old gauntlet of declaring that any barriers they face are simply a communication challenge.

Take the example of a brand of toilet soap that wanted to re-invent itself by offering greater functionality, whatever that might mean for a soap bar. The problem was, it wasn't first to market with a category innovation – it had been superseded by a competitor who decided to launch an innovation as a shiny new brand – with great success. So the lead communication agency involved had a brand with negative imagery for toilet soap, no functional differentiation versus 'new brand on the block', and it was going to market at the same price point as the new player. The brand owner's team's view – not surprisingly, but very unfortunately – was to decide that advertising could be the point of difference, and justify the price point. The resulting work was radically different for the category – so different in fact that users didn't understand which product category it was for – never mind which brand. And the initial sales were abysmal. Whose responsibility was this? The client who issued the brief? Or the agency that accepted it?

The problem with these converts and fundamentalists is that they may be devoted, but they get only a tiny piece of the big picture. That may be good for the warriors, but what does it say about users? Who does one believe? In these circumstances, what does a better product or service mean?

If the ability to identify highly subjective perspectives and manage them diminishes, either through lack of experience or the quality of relationships with people, the fortunes of service enterprises and brands themselves will be hostages to more highly narrowcast or biased perspectives. These kill brands.

Challenges to Objectivity – Numbers and Knowledge

These two areas of analysis and management could be treated separately, but they are often clumped together as convenient weapons to support meaningful relationships between brands and their users. Both subjects enjoy enormous attention and carry weight, both in terms of expenditure, and time. They are big business. Planning has also grabbed a gong as a thought leadership player, but perhaps this is becoming a tad tarnished in some quarters, where planning as a form of intellectual celebrity has overtaken rigorous thinking, and other disciplines are in rebellion against this often self-promoted status.

Let's be fair. Every generation, since the Stephen King and Stanley Pollitt one invented the notion of planning in the UK, has produced a handful of brilliant, insightful, and respected people who have made a difference, strategically, or creatively, through being able to distil things that would make a difference where no-one else was looking. This has been Planning's high ground in claiming credentials. Sadly, the claim does not carry throughout the practice, and it still remains only the gift of a few exceptionally talented people. Planners should be treated like all other specialists. It is not the function which delivers. It is the individual.

Some clever people have spent a lot of time turning their thoughts to research-based ways to add value to the expensive business of building brands, and quite a few along the way have been handsomely compensated for their efforts and contributions. In some cases this may not have been entirely divorced from their attraction towards the significant compensatory aspects of these special areas of activity.

Qualitative researchers, as a specialist sub-group, have produced almost as many theories and applications as their own number to account for their ability to interpret what the traditional 'six housewives from Manchester' are going on about. Some of the more entertaining ones have ranged from latter-day Freudian models – "er, the uptake of credit cards among the downmarket groups is a function of their dependence on the mother-dominant cash factor", through to the purely semiotic – "the steps on the packaging embrace the idealism of the aspiration of Jacob's ladder in terms of the functional desirability of the software."

Here we see influential people, who are supposed to deliver objective reports on what ordinary folk told them about what was placed in front of them delivering something else altogether. Are we missing something?

Imbalance, impressionism, imprecision, presented as some form of objective knowledge often dominate interpretation. Perhaps it's the creativity of the interpretation that's being paid for. Imbalance may well be accidental, yet so many times you'll hear people say, "That's not what was said in my group". Was the exclusion of what they heard an appropriate piece of editing?

A planner came back from watching most of the groups in a particular piece of research convinced the agency had a great idea. There were some issues about details of execution, but not serious ones, and in the chat after the groups the researcher said they couldn't envisage any problems with proceeding. In the debriefing the researcher, in response to a direct question from the client, stated that he did not think the client should pursue the idea. There was no evidence from the groups to support this view – on the contrary, users responded well both in terms of intended take-out, and style. Was this an impressive piece of interpretation, or simply a case of the researcher not liking the idea?

The communications agency lost the business. Maybe fair, maybe not. But the highly subjective was definitely at play.

Impressionism refers to that group who understandably want a further job and so paint a scene they wish the research commissioners will feel comfortable with, as opposed to saying "the women thought your idea was rubbish, and said so."

Take the example of a research debrief on a piece of stimulus material for advertising a new food product. Very circumspectly, the research agency indicated that the idea was not understood, did not communicate, wasn't really liked, but thought there might be potential in the music track. Everyone nodded. The planner then asked whether it wouldn't be more appropriate to start again, all things considered. The research agency was very reluctant to agree to this, until asked why they thought a music track constituted an advertising idea, when they capitulated. When asked two weeks later, over lunch (in those days people used to hold meetings in restaurants) why they hadn't just said the idea wouldn't work, they said "We thought it was too late in the creative development process to say that." In fact the reverse is true. It doesn't help anyone to find out two weeks before a scheduled shoot that an idea sucks. Those apoplectic at the challenge to their integrity can also rant at the market research societies who will protest their rigorous standards and codes of conduct. For some researchers, objectivity is a word that represents a gift in the same way that 'reasonable' spells significant revenue for interpretative lawyers.

And imprecision? Well, exactly. How can you ever be precise in such a complex scenario as a set of qualitative research groups? And in particular, how can you be sure the respondents are telling the truth? From our own direct experience, we offer a couple more points to illustrate.

One of us is sitting in the office. It's 4pm on a Tuesday afternoon, and the phone rings. It's a good friend who lives in South East England. After the "How are you/when are we going to catch up?" chat, he gets to the point. "Am I going to be moderating any groups in Kent that evening on dog food?"

"No," I respond, "Why?"

"Oh well, I'm going to be a respondent in one tonight, that's all."

"But you don't have a dog," I respond.

He says "I'll be thinking about what it would be like if I did."

On another occasion, we were involved in doing some research on a domestic utility in the London area. We thought we recognised one woman from a group the previous week, only because she stood out when the whole group had sympathised with her as she admitted to everyone that she had a very serious cleaning phobia, and we all empathised with her. So the next day, back in the office, we called the recruitment agency and asked them to check. It turned out that five of the eight respondents had been in the research project we had been conducting the previous week. Of course we could be criticised for not noticing, but that's not really the point.

Increasingly, users display a disturbing fluidity and facility with marketing departments' use of business school language, or directing a conversation in a way they think might entertain us.

It's not their fault. Recruiters are paid very little, so why go to the bother of finding virgin respondents, who don't talk anyway in groups – why not serve up people who have an opinion? But more to the point, if we persist in viewing users under a microscope as objects to be observed, we don't deserve any better. As Schrodinger noted, the very act of observation changes the observed.

Many people think they are giving great value for money in this field, and there are plenty of clients who feel they're getting their money's worth too. Look at all the advertising effectiveness papers that talk about the platforms for fresh insights that research created. A lot of hard work has gone into trying to achieve a scientific level of robustness in this area, yet these kinds of papers are few in number, and they too often try to edit out high levels of subjectivity in the actual trail of getting to a result. It is often this absence of genuine objectivity, scientific method, or other external reference points that account for the rise of the seers whose confident pronouncements are taken as gospel.

Let's put a little test question into this arena to see how robust all this stuff is. How many times have you ever heard a planner say another planner was right all along, or better than they are, if they've just been asked to take up a piece of business from an incumbent?

"No, you don't need me on that business, the last planner got the job right, there's nothing for me to do." Far too many times, weeks, months, even years are devoted by the new arrival to killing a legacy, not always consciously. In consort with brand teams who are also trying to create fresh scar tissue on otherwise healthy brands, they comply to slow down progress, because they believe they would suffer in their careers for apparently doing nothing other than getting on the with the job of finessing something that had already been done perfectly well. Planning is not a team game, at least not when it comes to working with other planners. The other version of this is the implicit message "That can't be right, I wasn't working on it."

What unites these kinds of planners and researchers is their ability to reinforce what is becoming an institutionalised piece of behaviour. This responds to the projection that "We may be so close to our brand that we can't be objectively sure as brand managers what people really think about our brand, so we'd better get some gurus to be objective for us", and the gurus tacitly acknowledge the set-up, manufacturing ever-more complex views on how all these brand-issue-things are difficult to divine, and so how much more essential their own unique contribution to comprehension, salvation, and increased compensation is going to be. This is anathema to the pure-at-heart who are trying to do a fine job, but for others it is how they see their role and contribution.

Like the old and now therefore to be derided One-Minute Manager-type books, does anyone ever hear a planner catching another one doing something right? "What's right with this strategy?" Fresh thinking is one thing, but it doesn't always have to be coupled to an attitude that excludes all other contributions, past or present.

It's no better in those quantitative research presentations people have to give so much time to attending. When you come up with a sensible question, how often does the response sound like this? "Well, our findings indicate that from our overall averages you could expect this to be better, but in fact you've raised something we're looking at, and we're refining the model to take that on board". How long do we have to wait for these refinements to be refined – and for what?

"Oh, the women didn't think the shampoo molecular demo-sequence was awfully gripping". Well, isn't that surprising? But why is it better to hear that after spending thousands of dollars on a preview test? Does high expenditure on research equate to truth? Too many people involved with brands and communications fall foul of the old seduction that since it costs so much to build and maintain brands, everyone had better have great insurance before trying to add a new storey to the brand tower. Try telling that to a good idea, which can't discriminate in those terms. This approach also says "Hey, you'd better get me mega-bright things on board because, you know, this is intellectual and expensive and you (morons) need help".

There is no shortage of material on what good planning and research can do in the right hands but it's swamped by bad research in the wrong hands, expensively reinforcing the Pavlovian reaction "Let's go to research". Maybe there should be a few more people brave enough to say. "Well, before we research this, what are we trying to find out?" before opening the order book. Or even, "What does the research we've already got tell us?" Collecting all the data in the universe doesn't help if no-one can usefully interpret it.

It's a human phenomenon, but nonetheless true, that many planners and researchers want to re-invent the wheel. In our experience, there are enormous amounts of valuable data already existing within client companies that no one ever looks at. The preference is to do it all over again. This is great news for the research companies, but a really bad use of time and money and knowledge. Many planners are allergic to anyone else's strategy – but professional researchers ought to know better

Take the example of a big multi-national trying to roll out a successful 'meal-aid' product across Europe. Given UK meal habits, where families don't eat together, and everyone eats different things, it's all about convenience and it obviously didn't make sense to try to export a UK-based strategy to a market where the family meal still meant something. So the product was launched in such a market on an ad-hoc basis as a treat for young couples, and really struggled for reasons of both siting in-store, and lack of user acceptance of the need for different cooking methods to get the most out of it. It was de-listed after just two years. No one had thought or wanted to look at the Nordic market where the product – with just three flavour variants – performed very well based as a mid-week treat for the whole family. 'Not invented here' is alive and well.

Planners and researchers really ought to be as objective as they like to think they are, but there is still far too much left to subjective interpretation, or editing, to lead to neutral observations. An awful lot of money is being wasted.

Research that may lead to a razor blade being more effective, a diaper being more absorbent, a digital camera being sharper, a battery lasting longer, a drinks can being easier to open – nothing wrong with that.

Spending £500,000 researching advertising that is driven by the imposition of tired formulaic clichés by rapacious brand teams, blind to real user needs, hiding behind company communication codes, is a total waste of the money previously teased from those most insulted by this behaviour – the very users of the brand. If that sounds harsh, think again of the sums involved – half a million pounds is still a considerable amount of money.

Too many people spend far too much time trying to get words down on a piece of paper entitled 'Strategy', and far too little time asking themselves the question "Would I, or anyone I respect, buy this product if I was looking at it this way?" Just how many of these kinds of statements can you really buy into?

- It doesn't just lift your mood – it makes you a better person (from a brand of coffee).

- Use this product – and you'll feel great (from a box of washing powder).

- Try this shower gel – and you`ll look and feel great.

Unless of course you're a crusading brand warrior, in which case you'll recognise what's being said here and demand more of it. It's a brand manager's version of a suspension of disbelief, the kind that eventually gets you promoted for dedication and commitment.

And there's one more thing we should ask ourselves at this point. Are we really listening to what the consumer says? It has become a commonly repeated mantra that 'the consumer is king' and that communication is a two-way process, and that we need to be in a dialogue with the consumer. And to give credit to the market research industry, we see the creation of many new tools, often online now, which do enable a proper two-way conversation.

The trouble is that they are still not the norm. If you are a brand-owner, it is difficult to let go of the comfort blanket of normative data. Unfortunately, much of this has been collected based on the old 'command and control' model of consumer research. We ask the questions, you give us the answer (we are looking for).

So the issue is, "Are we hearing what the consumer really thinks? Or are we still collecting the responses we want to hear?"

It is past time for us all to embrace a more inclusive approach to research, to engage the consumer in a dialogue and understand both what they are saying and why. Today`s consumers are not morons. As David Ogilvy famously said, "The consumer is your mother", and it`s time we paid more than lip service to that again.

Our brands are not the centre of our universe. Not even close. We need to understand brands' roles in our lives and act on it. How can we help real people go about their day to day lives more pleasantly and easily rather than intruding upon them? Planners & researchers have a key role to play here.

Planning is supposed to include the ability to ask the right questions – not simply pontificate about a product or brand based on superficial or highly subjective levels of understanding and analysis. Separate wisdom from questionable proximity, otherwise known as can't see the wood for the trees, as the planner pronounces about a day-to-day shampoo, "Well, my trichologist says..."

Planners should be there to strip back the gloss, not pile it on. And since when was the role separated from the other parts of the 'service value chain' in not being held responsible for the outcome of all this marvellous input? Let's face it, superb planners look set to remain a rarity for some time to come. Some of those including themselves in this scarcity descriptor should recall that Rembrandt only painted 234 works, yet 483 of them are in the US alone. If people can get around the growing tendency to over-intellectualise, and bring clarity to challenges, they would make a far more valued contribution. If they focused on just five questions, more of them could be or remain stars:

- What is the best thing we can say about this brand today?

- Is what I am saying credible? – Can I justify it?

- What kind of difference to the business will it all make?

- How is it really relevant to our customer?

- Is it expressed as clearly and simply as possible?

In getting to the Oscars, the planner should also ask whether they themselves really understand how the recipients of their wisdom will think and feel about the brand and its proposition. If you think the idea you have helped generate would never appeal to you, are you right to presume it will appeal to those you are presenting it to? "But I'm not the target audience", is a response that can be dangerously close to being wrongfully patronising. Difficult but also worth reflecting on is the question - should you be the planner on this brand anyway? Great planners know their limits.

David Ogilvy himself began his communications career as a market researcher with Gallup. It's time more planners and researchers reached a perspective that concludes that appropriate levels of simplification in managing multifaceted brands and businesses are more valuable than over-intellectualisation. There is too much of a fetish for complexity.

> What is the best thing we can say about this brand today?
>
> Is what I am saying credible – can I justify it?
>
> What kind of difference to the business will it all make?
>
> How is it really relevant to our customer?
>
> Is it expressed as clearly and simply as possible?

New Product Development

What are some of the effects of subjective impacts, this time on the new product development (NPD) process? This, the fresh lifeblood for many operations, comes at a price, some 80% suffering a short-mid-term death-rate.

How you choose to regard this is critical. It depends on your culture, your perspective, and often the compensation context in which you find yourself. "The twentieth century was awash with inventions and innovations, so that most had to fail. Recognising this will have a liberating effect....Indeed the key problem in research policy should be ensuring that there are many more good ideas, and thus many more failed ideas"[1].

There are those companies that try to institutionalise an innovation process, others that spend a fortune on blue-sky sessions, still others that trust to blind faith. Quite a number don't even exercise much judgement at the early stage to kill weak ideas. Oh yes, there are always plenty of naysayers along the way, which is why you always get those "there aren't any rules" and "don't be negative" intros from the fun fanatics and the "let's all take our shoes off" facilitators. They're usually smiling because they represent companies who are taking wheelbarrows of money a session for essentially providing flip-charts and post-it notes to a group of self-helpers who end up doing all the work anyway. "We think it would be just wonderful to have big balloons full of shower-gel to let off over pop-festivals when it's raining so you can wash all the mud off" – and thank you.

Before the disbelievers and anti-cynics step up, it's timely to remind ourselves that all these examples have actually happened. We don't have to make things up because you can always find wondrous things in reality. The energy and enthusiasm is amazing, but often it's linked to huge amounts of waste, like old energy generators – coal gives off little heat in relation to the energy expended in its consumption.

Whatever the new development processes, there always seem to be organisation and cultural barriers to making smooth headway in a competitive time frame. Engineering companies often feel uncomfortable with soft concepts, emotionally-led ideas, even if they're allegedly selling products in the toiletries and personal-care sectors. They feel even less comfortable with products that don't spell out their rationale for being. In the wrong hands, products which did manifest these characteristics in the olden days would almost certainly now meet early deaths today, being judged irrational under the subjective eyes of their managers peering out from their rational comfort zones. What they might have insisted upon:

- Gordon's Gin – "It's the unique blend of botanicals that give it a special flavour."

- Disneyland – "We engineered Mickey Mouse into a safe leisure environment for you and your whole family."

- Chanel No 5 – "Only the finest ingredients designed to harmonise together go into each bottle."

Could the actual products have come out of a brief which said "Give us a gin we want to drink, make magic more magical, celebrate charisma," in the hands of the modernists?

The engineers want to engineer and want tangible materials to work with. It is often impossible for some of them to work, as they would put it, backwards to create products from words or ideas that inspire others to action, like dreams.

Others find it difficult to uncover paradoxes that they can resolve, such as gentle efficacy, improved immortality, and exciting safety – think of the products which deliver these. Examples like this include aloe vera, digital photography and video games.

On the other hand, many people with the word 'creative' on or near their job descriptor often cannot make ideas concrete either – "Let's have something more wishful: the brief is 'blue – jealous – wicked'. Turn it into something tangible." Eyebrows get raised, people shift uncomfortably in their seats, they suddenly come over all rational and say, "What's that supposed to mean? That's not a brief".

If you can find people who are able to act as translators, or as bridges connecting these different kinds of behaviours, approaches, languages, and styles, then both kinds of parties can produce lasting innovations, but it's not just about throwing people together in an off-site brain-storm. Idea-generating teams need to be cast carefully, and they need sharp tools to do the job.

Much of the complexity that exists in day to day business exists because many marketing practitioners find it difficult to translate what theory means into normal behaviour and actions. Finding people who can do this is key, and key to improving is necessary simplification coupled with action in the here and now.

Sometimes, just getting to the engineers, having got past the layers of protection they get from other departments, can lead to surprising results. For example, ascertaining there might be a market for a more sensual kind of shampoo, discussing how engineers and labs might produce the right thing from their extensive existing knowledge, they said, "Of course we can – let's just take x and y and there you go." The point is, neither the marketing party nor the engineering party in this case would have got a result through their existing NPD methodologies, and a wacky all-hands-on-deck brainstorm environment with little structure wouldn't have generated the release mechanism either.

So more often, our R&D colleagues could connect with our users directly – it can have surprising results.

Imagine a food technician going around a supermarket for the first time with a 'real life housewife'. We were horrified to realise that one of these specialists had never considered that mums buy everyday food on price, and even more horrified that this revelation took up two hours of discussion in a brain-storming session.

Or think of the hair technologist hearing women talk about the fact that they don't really care about how their products work, just as long as they do. Although new claims will drive trial, they won't sustain repeat purchases unless the product delivers on their terms.

Another classic emerges from the fear of new proposals destroying old ones, and possibly the jobs that go with that, real threats which rarely emerge from the blue-sky environment, yet which tacitly drive behaviour.

An electronics company was busy developing voice-recognition technology in one place, and was making remote handhelds for TVs in another place. "Why not make a voice-recognition remote?" Well, the handheld boys rejected this because it would change what they were doing in ways they couldn't face, that is, job losses. The voice-recognition boys also rejected the idea, saying they couldn't develop a sufficiently all-embracing recognition package to meet the needs of markets, this from a group who helped to voice-automate the timetable enquiries service for the Swiss rail network, who presumably have more than one customer. Neither party was willing to interfere with a status quo, or accept an idea outside their domain, or try something new which could have been competitive for a new generation. People seem to deliberately forget that in new technology NPD, things start simple – you rarely launch with the omega product version. The iPhone bears little resemblance to the Racal mobile we first saw in 1987. If that was the case, we'd still be waiting for an awful lot of ultra-developed products to appear without their eagerly awaited but stumbling predecessors. At some point the iPhone 9 is going to appear quaint.

In some cultures you just have to come to terms with the fact that there are tectonic shifts that cannot be comfortably embraced. Component creators couldn't quite stretch to accepting how they could get a comfortable and consistent return from an investment in, say, a *Mr Bean* movie, which is demonstrative of how Philips and its Polygram portfolio eventually came to part. The adage, 'horses for courses' needs to be taken into account.

A reluctance to try something is equally countered by the "It's from us so it's the best" syndrome, which accounts for other countless damp squibs. Why would anyone want to buy an over-engineered mobile phone with a one and a half hour battery life and a tendency to crash often? Well, enough for a few thousand people to buy one, once.

Why do company people still expect users to worship at brand altars? We'll come back to this again later, but as a beginning, here's a typical example. "This product will be at the centre of your 'kitchen experience'." Hey, it's powder in a packet, and there are still plenty of insecure housewives out there, so they say. But there's another dimension to all this as well. There's no accounting for the behaviour of people in response to new products and services either. It's all very well to introduce an electronic diary for adolescent girls, "because they keep diaries", but not if you knew girls weren't remotely interested in electronic gadgets like these, or not then, in the mid 90s.

ATMs were a good idea. After twenty years of queuing to get your own money out of a bank from the one teller who was working on a Friday lunchtime taking cash receipts predominantly from local shopkeepers, along comes the hole-in-the-wall. Yet today, and especially at weekends on high-streets, you'll see twenty or more people in line, displaying no signs of distress, waiting to get their money out of a machine, while their now open bank is empty, and the teller sits there doing largely nothing.

We are now apparently happy to pay a premium for the fancy little stalls and counters within megastores that give us the personal service those same megastores took away years ago in their drive towards choice and value. The next development will be the sponsorship of supermarket villages with little shops run by tenanted families selling a variety of goods under themed elements. It's what we used to call a village, and what in Italy today is called business as usual.

New product development is also the pursuit of celebrity. For many it is akin to the thrill of the casino, the chase, the extreme sport. For others it's a careful risk averse process, full of trepidation and checks, but in both approaches, the driver or motivation is the un-stated acquisition of personal success, reputation, recognition, respect, remembrance, the offering up to those grand acquisitors of new badges, new toys to display.

When you walk into a shopping area and see the fourth or fifth shop selling a niche product, you know you are about to see a bubble bursting – whether it was skateboards or shares, ice-cream or coffee, unless you are in a souk, where the very focus of many sellers of the same goods creates an altogether more wholesome standard of quality and choice for the customer, and fewer fads. By this stage of experience and development, the early successful entrepreneurs have exited.

4. Living in the Real World: the Convergence of the Old and the New

Let's look at other factors that are impacting on how we interrelate with brands today. Some of them are current, others we have to go back a few years in time to really understand. First of all we take the current phenomena – fame, respect and the pull of celebrity.

Fame and respect are two kinds of tokens which appeal differently to different people. In an individual's mind they can add up to something desirable which wants to break beyond Andy Warhol's dictum that in the future "everyone will be famous for fifteen minutes". With brands, in the drive towards securing a place in history, there is still often a tendency to try to breathe more life into precious new products than can be reasonably borne out.

The tension between making one's mark, another form of personal branding, and the objective value of the marker, can lead to crazy and unsustainable propositions, which an occasionally vulnerable user group will play along with, sometimes for a long time.

In a world where most major companies have not existed for more than a few decades, the temptation to develop one's celebrity must be irresistible for many. Of the five hundred largest US companies in 1957, only seventy four were still part of that select group, the Standard and Poor's 500, forty years later. Only a few had disappeared in mergers, the rest either had shrunk or went bust. Understand that whatever the plea to sublimating self to the greater good of the resilient brand, the principal reason for inflicting that line extension or innovation on the world at large is about that highly politically charged subject called self-aggrandisement, of the personal or corporate brand kind. The brand is there to enable you to draw attention to yourself within the highly respectable company's codes of practice. Of course, the brand is bigger and better than any one of us, but boy can it be persuaded to play a key support role in Brand Me.

Senior people in companies still get involved in brand communications, the rationale being "because it's a significant cost/investment" or "I have to be very close to ensure we respect the brand's values." Who's going to say "Over my dead body will that ad appear because it will make me look like a dork at the golf club?" The closest cliché we usually arrive at is the "My wife/secretary/husband doesn't like it" response, which in some cases may be a lot more worthwhile than the £500,000 conclusion the brand group got to with its entourage of courtly research partners. On the other hand, if it works out, it's not a bad ribbon to add to the campaign medals, and maybe even a few more people will be able to associate what you do with a brand or company they've now heard of.

These days, ambition and self-seeking are smothered in politically correct phrases, so trying to make benign the kind of behaviour we have always seen before but clearly incorrectly ascribed. Not shouting or swearing while you get to the top is simply a style variant. Maybe those who don't make it feel better because no one ever raised their voice at them. Oh and it's OK not to be at the top either. Getting everything done nicely, with appropriate levels of 'dignity in the workplace', implicitly assumes that everyone is able to buy into and participate in the same system.

Unfortunately, not everyone shares the same values, and some will try and rock the boat. These types often end up as the people others revere as leaders. Leadership doesn't always come in the form of fireworks, but it also rarely comes from those who only sport never-broke-a-rule badges. And don't forget, many pre-selected leaders were permitted to rise in environments where their peers were granted no such freedoms. Once you've been chosen, sinning is OK. If you're not chosen, try and find somewhere where you can be, or someone who will choose you. Favouritism is a function of being human.

Communication ideas only live if they pass the favouritism parameters of the approver. Not knowing what they are leads to surprises, not always of the pleasant variety. While it is as bad to write things like commercials in a certain way to assure good 'pre-test' research scores as it is to write for the known preferences of the approver, repeated attempts to get people to change their world views on the back of a mere advertising execution alone are doomed to failure as well.

In fact, it's surprising how many ideas ever get made, broadcast, narrow-casted or printed, the chances of them fertilising an approving recipient being extraordinarily low in procreative terms.

There are times when a good run on getting great ideas out is heightened. These can coincide with the establishment of new or breakaway companies. At other times excellent work results from a combination of courageous clients and confident agencies, such as the legendary VW work in the US, and long-running campaigns for products like Absolut or *The Economist*. Then there are times when individuals create pieces of thinking that help create breakthrough ideas for a period, beyond any specific creative execution talent they have. For example, there are those who developed strategies of disruption, like the advertising legends Messrs Dru or Seguela in France, or those who convinced people to zag when others were zigging, like Steve Jobs, or those who try and differentiate through deeper questioning, like the old Rosser Reeves 'Unique Selling Proposition' approach, or the age of 'Positioning' from Rees and Trout. These are often backed by some, or all, of the following circumstances: a

- supportive management

- desperate management

- owner/driver management

- new product launch

- product getting little attention

- changed team

- savage competitive onslaught

- category code changing insight.

Many of the change agents are beyond the control of just one or two people, yet they have a major impact on who gets to work on projects, and how ideas are progressed.

The 'creative' environment

We have argued that the desire for fame is a pervasive and powerful factor in the buying and selling of communication ideas. But before an idea ever gets that far it is developed and discussed by people in the environment of some kind of creative agency – and the wider world is forcing change here too. New media, new channels, an empowered consumer, all are causing a cultural clashes or mismatches. Established ways of working are being re-evaluated, new ways of communication explored. There's no safe way forward anymore, and old areas of expertise are no longer necessarily accepted. It's not a comfortable place to be, but it's the same place it's always been. Those who like it and are being rewarded for going with it usually say there is no better time like now to be in the marketing communications business, the ideas business.

People have written about ways to get better new product ideas and communications, and they've produced checklists both detailed and worthy. But many, while acknowledging that the business of creating and developing ideas is for certain about ways of thinking about things, spend much less time on the cultural contexts in which those things are received and judged.

The elusiveness of it all is much more about the point that the delivery of successful ideas is just as much a function of trying to manage the psychology of the companies that create them and buy them, so often creating riddles about how the dynamics of such organisations operate.

If the generation of new ideas is embedded in the operating culture, like it legendarily once was in 3M, and closely allied to compensation systems, or if the approach to innovation has been revolutionised, like it has at Procter & Gamble, the chances of breeding further sustained success are enhanced. In too many alleged creative enterprises the right to be creative is tightly restrictive and protected, and there is little reaching out to people who may be able to provide fresh and innovative insights.

"Branding isn't about products, it's about perception."[1]

This observer said that when a product is unable to be the best in terms of either quality or value it faces an uphill struggle to convince users of its merits. In the same book he also quoted Harley Davidson as a failure in terms of trying to extend its franchise into perfumes, but otherwise a winner. We would suggest that in a competitive context its value is almost entirely about engineered perception. The end result may be the same, but the way of getting there is entirely different. There are lots of case studies on Harley and how the brand's iconic status evolved, one of which cites Ronald Reagan's desire to transform America's gunfighter character legend into a heroic figure that could "salvage the country's traditional values."[2] Harley's Steel Horses were the ones this figure was supposed to demand to ride. The study also points out that Reagan imposed significant tariff increases against imported heavyweight motorcycles and power-train assemblies (from 4.4–49.4%) to protect Harley's business. This is a different business from managing intrinsic quality or value. It is hugely more about managing perception.

Perception management will embrace a wider range of ways of engaging potential users of brands than before, where continuous physical product improvement or clearly differentiated value has peaked.

It is not advertising itself that will die, it's just formats and descriptors that will change and mutate, as the coming generations, who are brought up in a predominantly visual image world, will tire of constrained structures like time-lengths for commercials. The decline of the traditional 30 second commercial and the rise of, say, on-line-based PR, or a shift in balances, will happen because more and more people are working on concepts that implicitly acknowledge that brands are about the quality of the relationships we have with them, and traditional advertising structures may no longer be as sure-fire a way to nurture these connections as they once were figured. Furthermore, television advertising of the mass broadcast variety can't talk to people in real ways both because rules and regulations won't let it, and because it does not always provide consumer-relevant information – and people know that. It's 'out there', but at least more and more brand users understand its codes and operating parameters these days.

The real issue for a number of creative directors in places that cannot embrace changes at a realistic pace, all too often, is, "What added value can their perspective bring?" Beyond specific, focused brand companies, like fashion houses, or technology focused enterprises, like Apple, it is a rare thing to spot a creative director who has the range of experience or motivation broad enough to be truly objective and insightful across many different products, channels, and mind-sets. Can traditional creative hierarchies really work in these environments? Is it fair to expect them to? Imaginations are different. What exactly is being managed here? What does the sole creative director really represent - the organisation, the client, the user, an ego? When is it time to move on? What identity should such a person have? What should such a one say 'no' to? It is not surprising that many creative directors abandon direction and return to idea generation, or get burned out and move on. There is often too much to sustain. There remain a small group of heroes who transcend most barriers and sit blessed in the recognition and respect of a kind of hall of fame around the world, but again, this is a case of exceptions not rules. Like with planners and planning, creativity is about individuals more than a function. Nurturing this kind of subjectivity can bring great dividends, but it is often nurtured in the wrong way, as we will demonstrate later.

We've looked earlier at the way metaphors often fail to translate into execution, and here's another list of some of the folks from old worlds who've been inveigled into the creative service of just one brand category that has received years of interest and scrutiny: Heraclitus, Plato, Zeus, Apollo, Aphrodite. Yes, it's soap powder again.

Modern society has done much to make previously lauded cultures kitsch in the pursuit of commercialisation.[3] There are still plenty of people around trying to fit or stretch brands into mythologies and parallels that may be intellectually comforting but don't really add to a brand's chances of a long-term profitable existence.

Yet we know the appetite for doors of perception remains, as brand managers try to fashion new keys to open the treasure chests of the brands they are the brief custodians of. So if this brand is Apollo and that one is Aphrodite, where does that leave the user? Well, nowhere actually. Because managers have still frozen her in time, in a perspective that locks her up as the mother/cleaner/carer for her darling family, freshened in the eyes of the marketers by the introduction of the twenty eight year old son still living at home. This is cryonic management.

What misguided thinking has managed to last so long that many managers almost compulsively believe people should still conform to these stereotypes?

It has taken generations for people to even begin to see that the role of brands is in the context of how you conduct your life in general, not in terms of how you serve the brand's view of your role in its world. We continue to struggle with this today. It's extremely hard to accept that other people i.e. consumers in some cases might actually be "in charge" of your brand in the real world today. That doesn't mean they design it, but it does mean they contextualise it realistically.

In this other world, the real one, no one would think how to tell you that if you thought a new packet of powdered soup or sauce would transform your life that day you should get a life. But brand management folk and their suppliers spend their days, months, and years going over the same old ground and hoping beyond hope that there's still going to be an audience out there to subscribe to this nonsense. Products, and their messages, need to evolve to survive. That doesn't mean they have to get more and more complicated to survive. They need to be reformulated, repackaged, reconstructed, and re-positioned to ensure they still have relevant appeal when other newcomers or equally revamped products emerge. It took ten years for successive managers not to understand that the use of rich lathery soaps in Europe had been overtaken by events in the users' mind, or that the possible creation of food that tastes great may have something to do with the displacement of the stock cube as the principal meal and family well-being saver.

Ah, you say, but people know how to decode ads, so while they know they can't actually drive a new car on an empty road, short of moving to Newfoundland, they accept that it's better to see this happening than to show the usual city grid-lock. It's like freedom and the open spaces, as corrigible as the Marlboro Cowboy, who wouldn't enjoy much of either of those in New York today.

So if you know that they know that you know, why perpetuate these processes? We have rich inner lives and imaginations. We can build our own credible fantasies about why our choice of car is ours. There must be some wonderful imaginations out there, because it takes a different kind of perspective than Jeremy Clarkson's to work out how someone would want to be seen in certain forms of pressed metal out on the roads today. Maybe it's just all a ploy to help the South African film production business remain healthy as providers of locations for new car launches – which again is ironic given that outside a few key spots there aren't a lot of roads there you'd want to drive many of these dreams on.

Despite all the clichéd communications coming out, there is a universe of supplier imagination being applied to brands, from design companies and communication agencies through research companies, new media ventures, old media players, and pretty much anyone who thinks they should be the lead players in brand development. The basic talent is undoubtedly available – but we seriously question whether it is being applied to best effect in all but a few cases. We are not talking about energy and effort here. We are talking about relevance and effectiveness.

These days, most companies in communications, media, and design now claim to operate strategically, and the menu of the day usually has some variations on these elements in it:

- communications overview

- consumer insights

- brand review

- positioning

- strategy

- naming

- logo design

- brand language.

These same groups of people can execute most of this now in any tangible media, from boardroom brochures to bus tickets, from events to experiences. And they all say the same thing – they will do a better job of helping you stand out than the next guy – oh, and they'll do it with great integrity too. But it's still astonishing how many people then come up with a new positioning, or 'promise' statements that, if they faced up to themselves as potential users might, would reject out of hand.

How many of us have seen benefit statements which suggest that if you use product 'x' you will feel good, or perform better, or interact with others more meaningfully? We would venture to suggest that for many brands this approach is a largely meaningless emotional promise surfing on a functionality descriptor. It continues to be extremely common. In fact we would doubt whether most readers of this book could hand on heart say they have never been involved in a situation like this.

Yet we continue to behave as though there are people out there dumb enough to say yes to this stuff, every day. Is this wilfulness or ignorance, vanity or arrogance, or something else? Do brands have a strategic life in a parallel universe with its own language, which only marginally affects the way brands are eventually adopted by people? Often they apparently do, and this is inside the companies that make, manage, or serve them.

The classic wish-list is the summary of what people want a brand to do. Here is an example of what the communication expectations were for a 30-second piece of video:

The brand should reflect its credentials as a natural source of quality. The brand should respect its heritage as an inspirational source of Scandinavian purity and mildness. The story of the new ingredients in the range available must also reflect the naturalness and mild efficacy of the product, so any ingredient references must refer to tapping into nature as it is, not interfering with it or reformulating it. Any story or presentation must capture the values of the brand's heritage and previous stories, and at the same time capture the target audience's attention and desire to try the new variants(s). Standard product in use and consequent benefit shots must be featured, even if new signature shots are developed to add fresh interest to the benefit story.

That takes thirty seconds to read out on its own.

Never was the adage 'a picture is worth a thousand words' expected to serve its purpose more effectively than in this kind of environment.

Even more talent is wasted on trying to find clever ways to express a desire more succinctly in an attempt to make it 'single-minded', but which merely masks the remaindered initial desire. Once told to use no more than two words to sum up a brand in the face of impossibly complex demands from an account management group struggling to keep a client happy, a wry planner said, "OK, then, I'd say it's multi-faceted".

What do phrases like "maximise buy-in of the new product" mean?

Let's take an example from a multi-national client who prided himself on team involvement.

The communications agency takes a call to be told, "We need to discuss with a very small team where we go from here". The agency fields the account head and the planning director, to be met at the client meeting with seven clients, all of whom express different points of view about the role of creative work.

The senior client says "So we're all in agreement then?" And unfortunately the planning director says, "I don't think so. You've all said something different. What are we supposed to direct our creative people to do?" The client response? "Well, I would say we're in agreement on a sliding scale."

So what do they mean – and what can you do with this response anyway?

As we said before, you can't blame people for chasing easy money, so get rid of the jealousy quotient when it comes to looking at who is out there claiming the high ground. But you can certainly ask more probing questions about values and returns. Or at least try and ask open-ended questions. You may still be accused of challenging the client's authority, but then you are still able to make choices about whether to work with people like this.

What do we mean by values and returns? They change. They are not so totally tangible either, and we turn to them now.

It has taken generations for people to even begin to see that the role of brands is in the context of how you conduct your life in general, not in terms of how you serve the brand's view of your role in its world.

Culture, Behaviour and Expectation

In broadening our perspectives it is important to look at the impact of culture on behaviour and expectation, and of course the obverse, through recent history. There are insights into how such often implicit or tacit workings in society have significantly influenced approaches and attitudes to communications codes and techniques, and attitudes about values. There is a special significance in the 'lag' effects these produce when dealing with brand definition, roles, and emerging expectations.

There is a whole world of people trying to look forward, trying to provide advice, searching to find meaning in some kind of marketing 'ether'. In one case this could be about the impact of new technology or new communication channels and how to utilise them to get a better understanding of life or users, and how to get closer to them. A survey on mobile phone usage[1] as a speaking device versus a downloading device revealed that one of the reasons for the slow uptake of high usage, or increased usage based on engineered features, was not cost, although that had been a severe limitation factor for those not on corporate budgets. It was simply that, and especially for men, they just don't want to talk for that long. How long had we known that from experience?

On a light note, what's the scariest thing a woman can say to a man? "Let's talk". The survey also revealed that for many people, media channels quickly find their own levels of usefulness that were not foreseen – so text messages for intimacy and emails or other on-line postings for longer versions of expression came into play where things didn't "feel right" if they were said on the phone.

Who would have predicted the use of mobile phone cameras to witness muggings or stage 'slappings', the images then being circulated as trophies? That was the equivalent of the old urban myths and legends that used to do the rounds with young football fans. You know, the one about the hardness of older opposing team fans who allegedly sported necklaces of their victims' ears or teeth. But today the urban myth has become a photographically evidenced and inspired event. Tokenism doesn't need time and urban mythology to travel anymore, but of course its roots (sorry) are from the past, as any social anthropologist will testify on his mobile phone camera from the safety of his digital fortress. So there's an army of people out there trying to decipher what all this new technology might mean, but not enough people looking at what's right in front of them.

We have our doubts about the adage that needs remain constant, and only the ways of satisfying them change. There really is much to suggest that needs do change dramatically over time, in one's own lifetime, and at the same time in different parts of the world. Maslov's hierarchy captured a part of this, and subsequent models like Young & Rubicam's 'Cross Cultural Consumer Characteristics' work took it in a different direction. Inequalities between rich globetrotters and local paupers, young celebrity-seeking social networkers and retired voluntary wealthy hermits simply dramatise the scenarios. Extremes are more possible than ever, where you can be more or less connected and influenced than before, and you can be more than one thing from minute to minute.

Previously, in cultures where a strong military presence could hardly be avoided, certainly in most of the Western hemisphere in the first half of the 20th century, the seeping into civilian life of military matters and conditioning provided an almost ubiquitous life-extending opportunity for brands to enjoy high volume sales. For example, on a detailed but important scale, if you were to look respectable as a man, you were expected to have shiny shoes and shiny buttons. It was a world of uniforms and yet simultaneously clearly badged signs of status and differentiation, subtle differences within norms. Women were in small ways conditioned through peer propaganda to judge a man's suitability according to the gleam on his footwear. Or if a brass button didn't blind you as it caught the sun you were a cast off, a symbol of slovenliness. Shoe polish and brass polish (like Kiwi and Brasso) had regular branded places and usage in a proper household's inventory. Today's equivalent would be showing a clean pair of Nike heels or for that brief period, the daily replaced flip-flops in LA, and the dazzle of the sapphire glass of a Big Watch. Next year it will be something else, and there will be variations everywhere.

Household goods of the 'self-raising' variety were those days' equivalents of 'Love Marks'[2]. They supported the projection that you'd "never had it so good", and that being spruced up would dramatically improve your chances of picking up a productive (in all senses) partner rather than being dull and tarnished, left on life's shelf, not fit for living. These signs, these signals of 'polish' occur in every generation.

As the military presence waned on the streets, and eventually was banned for a time in England for active servicemen when the IRA realised what an attractive target uniformed soldiers were, other forms of uniformed yet differentiating badging took their place. In England again, groups called Teddy boys came and went, Beatniks were faded up and down, Mods and Rockers took front stage, Hippies and Skinheads paraded by, and ever more focused identity groups formed a long tail - Punks, Goths, Metalheads. Now soldiers are again encouraged to wear uniforms proudly in 'civvy street'.

In the early 90's in Italy you would see a new fashion uniform each winter. Young people one year would wear jeans, boots, and sheepskin jackets, and all would scrutinize the kind of label each item bore. People who couldn't afford the right label mugged others for their Timberland branded boots. Everyone knew two things: who was rich and not wearing cheap copies; and that to a one they were each and all an individual.

In the same country, when manageably sized mobile phones, or 'handies', as the Germans call them, came out, everyone had one and proudly displayed it. Many conducted elaborate conversations with people on phones that were simply mock-ups.

Whatever happened to hats? Look at old photos and see how prevalent they were. Old means about 100 years old here, so that is truly ancient for many today. They may not be as universal as they once were, but the baseball cap is a major replacement contender, and hoodies had a fleeting role as a latter-day sign of recalcitrance. One headmaster at an English school decided the best way to counter their wear was to make them compulsory. Headwear has now been joined by hair wear, and at least one pair of sunglasses. In all these cases the artefact on display is saying "Read me, and know something of who I am today, at this moment. Approach me, or stay away, if you dare". To borrow from old sources, it was ever thus.

Modes of dress are one thing, technologies another, you might say, but both are harnessed by people to support their lives, dreams and ambitions, to make statements. The decorated suit of armour is one, the ceremonial sword another, the Rolex, the iPhone, the Prada bag, and so the world rolls on with its messages and messaging accessories.

Tom Lehrer, the American satirical songwriter once said "Some very good songs came out of the Second World War, even though it wasn't primarily a musical". Wars are often cited as being major drivers of

72

change, and like change, they are with us constantly. Regard wars as shapers of the way societies see themselves. In Western Europe, particularly after the First World War, but gradually since then, the effect of war has had a deep impact on the bi-polarisation of society regarding religious beliefs and practices. Increased secularisation has been parried by increased levels of fundamentalism. Pope Benedict in 2007 said if it isn't Roman Catholic then it's not a proper church, with Roman Catholicism being "the one true Church of Christ". Sub sectors of society see war differently from others like never before, goes the commentary. War is seen as something to avoid, by others as a means of effecting change in their favour. Bankers are dispassionate. They merely profit from human nature and its ways. Was it not always like this? Why are we labouring the point?

In the world of marketing and brands we are living in a fresh period of conflict, or tectonic shifts, between attitudes and behaviour, towards and about them.

What came along with industrialisation and mass production constituted radical new levels of conflict. Let's take some highlights. First was the means to develop more radically the whole notion of consumption. This was a great opportunity for those who got in early on the ownership of production techniques to enrich themselves in ways that had formerly only been open largely to kings and potentates – welcome to the new rulers, and to the new acquisitors. Second came the realisation that production also gave the owner the means to prolong control of the form of the goods being produced, and not as much as the media makes out has this changed. Most people are still basically offered givens. They don't ask for or specify what they would like until a new technology or product surfaces that they then post-rationalise as an obvious thing to have, and then they get stuck into the detail. Even in the cases where people asked for improvements in products, services, or standards, these came back into the market much later, with as much of the cost of change passed back on to the user or the suppliers, who didn't have the clout to complain. Often change only came about through legislation or regulation. In this benign climate of making everyone's life better, came a third highlight.

This was the view that communications about products could also be mass distributed, borrowing from the techniques of religion and propaganda, which had reached new levels of sophistication by the end of the 19th century. Not only could more people be given precisely what producers wanted to give them, they could be told what to expect, and be grateful – "For what we about to receive, may the Maker make us truly thankful". Communications for brands followed formats of preaching that were unassailable and presumptuous, that constituted an arrogant cocktail. The only differences came in the choice of qualifiers or promises based on compliance, but implied threats of fire and brimstone for dissent or avoidance were almost equal.

Once large numbers of people had been basically educated, and a hefty proportion of those subjected to the actual or influential experience of military organisations, they were significantly more conditioned to respond to what they were told to do. As the early brand promises shifted from the monstrously preposterous to the frankly outrageous to the almost tolerably credible, those electing to remain outside the protection of brands were finding themselves ostracised. The non-deodorised, pale toothed, grey-shirted man and his let-me-down wife became leitmotifs of the pernicious consequences of being un-baptised by omniscient and ubiquitous Brands.

There was an intuitive understanding on the part of the Message Makers that people are biologically programmed to choose solutions to problems that they decide are in their favour[3]. The optimistic person who is told they have been diagnosed as having an illness that produces a mortality rate of 28% within five years and a 72% survival rate will be predisposed to focus on the latter statistic. Jerry Maguire, in the eponymous movie, on being told by the woman he wanted to date that his chances were one in a million told his friend "It's great, she said I'd got a chance in a million".

It's not for nothing that 80% of people believe they are better than average today.

Events that get relabelled history ensure that there are pendulum swings as wars and other disruptions cause shifts in attitude and behaviour and sensibilities. Setbacks about self-esteem, feelings about the 'reliability of the future' and other questions about authority, trust and meaning, come in new guises with every generation. It's just that some seismic events have a much longer influence than others, and they in turn play their influential role in the smaller scale events and the perspectives they engender.

After two world wars many still found solace in their version of God or the Church, but major cracks had appeared in the 'screen' version of what the regular popular religions appeared to be offering to cope with the world. "Much positive reinforcement derives from religion – warm and comforting feelings of being loved and protected in a dangerous world"[4]. This is inextricably linked to a proposition in answer to the question, "What ultimately explains the lust for Gods?" Religion provides substance which feeds on the benefits of promoting trusting obedience, by providing respected sources for things, and the way things are, in a tone, by and large outside the happy-clappy versions, that commands formalised levels of respect and demands obedience.

If you soften these kinds of demands slightly and increase the chances of rewards in the here and now, you are effectively paving the way for a series of lesser gods to have a role in making life more tolerable, and in managing uncertainty

For a long time these lesser gods have been called Brands.

Brands worked because they let us in a little further than angry and distant gods. In parallel to the shift in people moving towards alternative agents to God for solace and succour came the understanding borne out of Darwin's observations that there was no longer an absoluteness to the notion that it takes "a big fancy smart thing to make a lesser thing".[5] Idolatry grew as the pendulum swung again towards personifying inanimate objects as agents. It almost seems to be that we are wired up this way.

Brands make themselves ripe to intervene in our lives.

For decades most brand producers took the position that we were there only to consume their offerings, hence the growth of the term consumers, not to challenge their given credo. Brand worship was expected, and given. Brands filled many holes in the formerly comforting but worn blanket that major religions had produced. The self was seeking succour in fresh ways.

Religions themselves had been smart enough to package themselves up with rationales that had allowed them to embrace and then usurp the magic and witchcraft of the Middle Ages, to the point where George Michael might have summed it all up pithily as "Well you gotta have Faith".

Brands in their turn came to expect their own levels of loyalty and devotion. Brands became faith healers. To build loyalty brands offered their versions of indulgences. There were short cuts to the promised lands, at a price. We see a new generation of Luthers who have come to rebel against all this. Brand Pro-Testants.

Armies of researchers acting as brand parish priests went out into the fields to provide evidence to those on high, the managers and owners, that these new gods were attracting flocks of faithful worshippers. With such feedback it is easy to see how brand managers came to see themselves as possessing special skills, and inhabiting a level in the world that made them different, more insightful, entitled. Anyone challenging this position, this authority, was heretical. Anyone challenging the brand was poisonous, heathen, and deserving of a form of Inquisition or ostracism matching the severity of their crime. Of course the crime was severe, because attacking or challenging a brand was the same as attacking or challenging Faith itself. Philip Pullman might have argued in his trilogy Northern Lights that major brands are like Daemons – separating them from you was a crime against humanity, and not having them made you inhuman.

Religions have provided brand makers with plenty of materials to build and defend their positions. Perhaps one of the reasons some Islamists despise parts of the West is because they see Westerners behaving in an unenlightened state of idolatry, where there is no longer one and only one true God, but many brand pretenders.

Challenging brands is a dangerous business, but a necessary one, because the conditions for and the worship of them have changed. There is still a large gap between brand management expectation and users that is creating sustained dissonance and waste. Those who most recognise this will be better equipped to help move lesser gods from a totemic face towards markets to a more integrated and balanced relationship between providers and users. But be aware it is still a dangerous pursuit.

As with many things in life, when discomfort or unhappiness with the status quo are first uncovered, reaction and rejection take opposite and extreme views and positions – capitalism bludgeoned by communism, nationalism by globalisation, liberalism versus discipline. We are in such a period now in the world of brand and marketing evolution.

For decades, the high priests nurturing brands decided to preach that 'The Customer is King'. Not only did many brands parade this, they simultaneously practiced contempt for it in their real actions, attitude and behaviour. Some enlightened brand owners actually came to realise that in many instances the customer can't be king in any but a small number of respects. Between these challenging forms of operating a new balance has begun to emerge in some quarters. Customers may well be kings in expecting to be treated as equals in terms of attitude and service, but not when it comes to inventing radical products. If Sony had waited for someone to tell them they wanted to walk around the high street with little cassette boxes and headphones so they never had to be parted from the Bay City Rollers, we'd still be waiting. Same goes for the iPod. For mature companies today that survive, 'the customer is king' is now qualified to define the circumstances under which this attitude makes it worthwhile or not. This is an important qualifier, because it is dictated by the brand maker's attitude to what is being provided, and therefore cannot remotely be objective any more.

Customers are also behaving differently. In parts of some societies, religion as 'the church' is now a barely detectable microwave background radiation of life. For others religion is burgeoning and supports the rejection of heathen goods and practices in the very same societies. For many, there are new manifestations of faith in this context, and new brands to satisfy them.

"I am what counts," is one such new credo.

"The modern British person has a firm belief in the primacy of their own rights at the expense of everyone else's." [6]

The forms of shift have been analysed and identified as generational pointers, and while these often get compressed to almost fortune-cookie size a deeper look at the source data points clearly to the move towards a Missouri-like "Show me" state for many brand users today – show me what you can do, not let me worship at your feet. The onus has moved, the worship has shifted, and a brand now has to show 'Me' respect. So we are moving to a world where 'The Brand and I' as the managers' group in this manifestation is trying for a place in the context of the user's statement that it is "My World" that must be satisfied now.

The challenge for brands and their owners in this context is to find ways to exist alongside these kinds of new and powerful self-based faiths and religious equivalents, with all their individuality and variations. As we have observed, it is needs that are changing, fundamentally too, and the old ways of meeting them really do have to change as well.

The next movement of the pendulum will result in a shift in the balance between creators and users, owners and sharers. But as perception also reveals, it is difficult to envisage a state of perfect harmony, because every generation provides momentum for the pendulum. This is as true for corporations as users. There will always be shifts, fault-lines, time lags, creating tensions and new opportunities.

Trying to understand the ways in which these elements and movements affect roles like brand management also opens up new areas and ways of thinking about how to manage the nature and form of being connected more effectively and efficiently.

This is another path fraught with danger, and will again only initially be pursued by the brave. "The immense majority of intellectually eminent men disbelieve in Christian religion, but they conceal the fact in public, because they are afraid of losing their income." [7] How does it feel in the marketing department today?

So, in a *Mediated* world[8], we are witnessing currently an inflationary universe of 'I'.

"I know what's right".

In this world, everyone's already an expert, so brands' former unquestioned expert status is being eroded. Brands are fragmenting, and have different roles to play. Another way of looking at this is to say that brand roles as signifiers are also shifting. The 'I' or 'Me' is no longer borrowing associations from brands to define its self in their shadows. The 'I' is using brands as elements of a group of contributors to an 'I' which is bigger than any group of brands. Brands are like cells that are generated, used and rejected according to today's needs and the environment one faces.

The old Jesuit attitude of the church, "if I get them before they're six I've got them for life", translated into the brand manager's desire for lifetime loyalty or commitment is simply naïve today. Many brands are now switched as swiftly as opinions. And why not? Few brands provide consistent competitive edges for lifetimes – their fortunes rise and fall. Fifteen years ago, who would have thought outside of Samsung that it would be cool, or that Hyundai would be the world's 6th largest car manufacturer, with quality products, by 2007? Notions of loyalty and longevity are changing as competition changes.

In the early days brands helped users manage their lives better in an uncertain world, because they offered many of the positives of religion with few of the extreme negatives. But as with most things that grow, from empires to icons, there comes a time when size, fame and fortune expose them to significant voices of detraction. Brands have often become victims of their own success. In some ways brands are less important than they used to be, and in others they are more important, as the modern ones replace more questionable sources of authority.

Whether one brand of lager or another is bought or not is not of any great consequence for the future welfare of the user,[9] and those brands that insist that their role is contrary to that will face extinction (yes, even in developing markets), or a slow lingering death. Like those self-important products, category advertising used to be amusing to watch. It was like the pop music business. We used to guess which year a pop record came out by identifying the sound of that year's must-have synthesiser or digital drum machine. At least one commercial music production company banned its musicians from using the pre-set sounds that came with new synthesisers just to try and get some original programming sounds into tracks to make a bit of a difference. With car ads you could spot the year of production from the number of helicopters that featured, or the number of cars seen ploughing through the water. The copy 'Follow Me' effect was legion. In many categories you could inter-cut slices of commercials for different products to make new seamless wholes the user couldn't see any differences in – they just disliked them all equally. But brand managements were proud, they were doing what the competition was doing, only better, they thought, and ring-fencing the category's story-telling capabilities and attributes.

In some markets witty communication agencies and brave marketing teams produced and bought advertising ideas that ironically transferred category clichés from one market to another, expecting the viewer to acknowledge the cleverness because they were supposed to be in on the advertising to the same extent as the creators, but only as recipients of the message. There was still little room here for the emerging 'I' to indulge. 'Follow Me' behaviour led to narrower and narrower tolerances for variations in best practice or established category codes. Car ads had close-ups of turning front wheels, soft drinks could only be dunked down by kids, detergent demos worthy of quantum physics lectures abounded, and a research industry complicit in checking for compliance compounded the narratives' restrictions.

Once in a while something would come along that would be briefly iconoclastic, then it would be diluted through mimicry. But the lists of awards for creativity and effectiveness have always been tiny compared to the mountains of dross that get dumped around them. Drone brands dominate. They create noise and clutter, not signals and clarity. What a waste of human space, not to mention time and cost. How did people start to escape from this bombardment of boredom?

Social networking sites have come to represent another celebration of the 'I' wishing to broadcast to all and sundry, and not merely sit passively in front of me-too messages. But research shows that users of networking sites are 'chronically unfaithful'.[10] There is little brand loyalty and no qualms about keeping several sites going at once. These sites also go to show that really motivating and engaging creativity with a decent half-life is hard to find. They just reflect the world of communications we've already seen, with 'I' – your name goes here – in front of them. Yet people are prepared to pay staggering sums to own these chimaeras.

For brand owners this means that some fundamental questions are going to have to be addressed, such as:

- What should my brand be like in the near future?

- Where can new sources of authority and reference come from, if indeed they are even requisites?

Sources of authority can come just as easily from the street as anywhere else,[11] and be just as easily undermined, or made to fade away leaving laggards high and dry with stocks of street-wise product everyone else has moved on from. Unless you are very swift, it is difficult to be a constant supplier to people who look in the mirror today and say, "Who's the coolest in the kingdom?"

The moment you've mastered windsurfing, along comes kite surfing. The moment you've mastered snowboarding, along comes snow-kiting, then it's back to a new variation of skis, and so on, leaving suppliers and equipment literally in the new multi-users wake. Of course many markets move more slowly, but the nature of the relationships between brands and users is moving in ways that affect a large number of brands. Those brands that cannot understand or see the shifts, and that are unable to take their new place in the users' reference system, are about to join the ranks of the recently departed, unless they too are of the lucky few that are selected for retro-status, prolonging their life in new ways for a while, like Kangol hats, or Dualit toasters, or Roberts' radios. The relationships these brands have with their users are of a particular type, which we shall come on to talk about, and not all brands can have them.

The sooner brands come to terms with the fact that they are increasingly a part of the context of people's lives, role players, bit part performers, not things that 'I' am attracted to, like iron filings to a magnet, the better the chance of building realistic levels of connectivity.

A brand may reveal the world it elects to live in, and invite people to sample it, but it is no longer relevant to try and imply that this is the dominant world you must depend on. That way madness lies.

Each of us builds, inside our head, a model of the world in which we find ourselves.[12] Where religion once offered consolation and inspiration, brands tried, and for quite some time succeeded in providing a portion of contemporary equivalents, as companions or confidants, but the onus is now on the brands to justify ways to remain preferred members of Our World, or My World. Not we be ruled by them. This is still not reflected in most communications, where we are contextualised in the car world, the banking world, the mortgage world, the washing world, the drinking world, the athletic shoe world, and so on.

Instead of "Join our Brand World", as it was, it is now, "See, Brand, if you can join My World". We live in a world beyond brands, as well as of them.

We will show you how you can reduce a dependency on the shackles of the past, and build profitable relationships with people based on values that are relevant for today. But it is only by understanding more deeply why we got to where we are today that we can see more clearly what to do about it.

In many cases, looking to a product's past to discover clues about its future can only result in disappointment if its cultural role and position are not understood in the context of the major shifts in the changing role of self in defining brands today.

The sooner brands come to terms with the fact that they are increasingly a part of the context of people's lives, role players, bit part performers, not things that 'I' am attracted to, like iron filings to a magnet, the better the chance of building realistic connections and relationships.

5. Seeing the Light – Living with Diffraction

One of the challenges of working with some brand owners is being able to provide insights without being killed in the process. 'Emperor's New Clothes' syndromes surround management teams and little children with untainted eyes are not especially welcomed. Successful brands are often managed by powerful and wealthy managements, or individuals. Some have a dedicated life inside their organisation and some have a life outside it. Sometimes these lives are separate, sometimes they are intertwined. Look at one example which puts a lot of emphasis on the outside – public altruistic giving.

What is known as the Potlach Effect is the scenario where giving to good causes becomes an advertisement itself of dominance or superiority, authenticated by cost.

"Individuals buy success through costly demonstrations of superiority, including ostentatious generosity and public-spirited risk-taking".

No longer the province of nation-state rulers alone, this activity is now in the province of Masters of the Universe. When these same people are in charge of the destinies of brands, they may be very successful all their lives, but some of them will also tenaciously hold on to the wrong position, or take the wrong direction, and for a while the business and its customers will profit, and then suffer.

You either need to be very confident and capable to manage these kinds of people, or comfortable coming to terms with the consequences. It is important to understand what kind of chance you have of affecting these scenarios, and the extent to which you might be able to introduce corrective lenses to improve the quality and condition of connectivity between the owners and users of brands in these circumstances. If lenses are there only to help the owner see his reflection better in the mirror, you need to decide what kind of organisation culture and climate you are most happy in. Some like to bask in reflected light, others like to shine a light to reveal new things. Sometimes there's enough light for everyone to enjoy the glow, or the rays. That's where we come back in. But not just yet.

One of the challenges for research with users in general is that human beings bring bias to decisions all the time, which can lead to very inconsistent results[1].

Scientific research shows our brain reacts differently to the same situation depending on how choices or selections are presented to us, and the fact that we cannot retain and use everything we know at the same time is the cause of bias. This means that we have arbitrary reference points and react to differences from those points. For example, when people are asked to estimate a number, they will position it with respect to a number they have in mind or one they just heard, so 'big' and 'small' are comparative. Decisions are contextually driven, just like brand choices.

Couple this with the fact that we may also be programmed to build a loyalty to ideas in which we have invested time, and the principal conclusion that can be reached from qualitative and quantitative research sources is that the information we receive is highly conditional.

Brands and their managers seek to condition us on the premise that our own loyalty will increase if we invest time with them, and that satisfaction will only occur if the time invested was sparked by motivating interest, or conditioned stimulation, in the first place. It's a neat circle.

Before religions were institutionalised, and formalised through corporations, what we call faiths, ideas and experiences were remembered because they were brought to life through compelling narratives – stories. Owners of religious brands learnt to capture, refine, and re-tell great stories. They had an intuitive feel for conditioning, backed up with sharp and painful objects to discourage narrative rejection.

Modern latter day brand owners adopted religions' empirical experiences and began to craft their own similar stories. But many failed to grasp that not every product under the sun can construct a compelling story, and that weak conditioning can be recognised by those exposed to multiple variants of the model constantly, especially if the conditioning isn't reinforced with harsh punishments. This is also increasingly true for people who have grown up surrounded by advertising messages and media.

So in the absence of an intrinsically compelling story, products sought to embed themselves in myths about life, which we are expected to find compelling because they touch deeper intuitions about experience. If the fit isn't too stretched, then these approaches can touch on our constructed view of the world, our respective perspectives meet, and a positive empathy may ensue. Brand managers of the past should be grateful they got anything like the levels of loyalty they aspired to for so long. Since our perspectives today are different, and we are more attuned to blatant models of conditioning, this approach will increasingly not work for many brands.

Remember also that it is only in the last decade that advances in disciplines like neuroscience, which is still not even recognised as a discipline in its own right in some academic quarters, have enabled us to get closer to look at the ways that things presented to us stimulate our brains/minds differently, and in different places.

In the true tradition of science, many researchers followed tried and tested paths, and suppressed Karl Popper's insight: "In so far as a scientific statement speaks about reality, it must be falsifiable; and in so far as it is not falsifiable, it does not speak about reality".

If they didn't know how to measure or capture something it was either dismissed as being absurd to attempt or ignored, and the current methodologies were advocated more vociferously.

So for years the ways people have really interacted with brands and responded to communications have been ignored, because they couldn't be captured and measured properly. Things were diffracted. We've been constructing incomplete worlds. As the cliché goes, what gets measured gets done, so an awful lot of expensive stuff has been done based on measurements that only resulted in half a picture being created. Let's call this the age of Flat Earth marketing and measurement.

We may not be able to predict the future from the past, but we can at least look there to see how we might have got a twisted view of the present. Lenses that do that can at least provide some corrective vision, and allow us to focus better on the way things really are.

Equally, models of distribution that have been enabled by computer capacity, across many fields, have allowed us to correct biases and build incremental businesses. This has led to analyses of markets that have gone against the grain, but which appear to be more common, or will be, than people dared to notice before.

Chris Anderson in *The Long Tail* pulled together a convincing case for some markets on the effects of increased choice and lowered costs on user behaviour, especially for digitally available products.[2]

The commercial aviation business is a good example of how real-time data and the ability to interpret it have created a complex market with another long tail. Once upon a time there was little choice, other than class of travel. Now you can fly with South West Airlines, Ryanair, Net Jets, and soon in your own VLCA jet, but few people are totally loyal to one form or experience. We are multiple users, and frame our experiences and judgements around that. The experience curve is simple. On our early flights, those we can remember, there was a thrill simply getting on a plane. Then the satisfaction gets into the detail – which class, which seat, real eggs or powdered, good air miles or not, bags arriving with you, none of the above. We credit or debit value on the providers as we transfer and compare experiences. What do we want today – First Class or Gulfstream, Big Plane or Bi-plane, MIG or balloon, helicopter, or parascending chute? Instead of passively responding to the providers' protestations about outstanding service we are ever more the ones who set the boundaries through the choices we make, or the choices our concierge services provide for us. In the same way we are multiple users, brands need to understand they are in multiverses [3] – they are no longer points of singularity.

Today you decide to ride your eco-friendly bicycle to the village shop, aware that it was made in the USA and flown to Europe. Does the ride influence your selection of a product when you get to the shops? Would your selection have been different if you'd driven to a shop in your Audi TT? These kinds of influences and choices have only been intuitively acknowledged in the past because there was no way of capturing information and analysing it on a large scale in a reasonable time period. More work can now be done on the quality and value of the interrelationships we have with multiple products and services than ever before. It's a new dimension that can be used to help create more dynamic and relevant relationships with and between users.

This will enable people to do what they do best anyway, which is to bestow trust and satisfaction on brands on their own terms, and for brand managers to get a better understanding of this dynamic.

Canny and caring users will also reward manufacturers and service providers with loyalty based on their corporate behaviour and attitudes, and reject them accordingly as well. Users can see into corporations' backyards and trash cans much more clearly than ever before.

So communications don't have to spend a disproportionate amount of their time demonstrating all the ways they are trying to say, "Buy me because you can trust me". 'Trust me' is the shorthand sentence in movies for the sign that things are about to go horribly wrong.

If we are wired up to like the visible, the personal, and the narrated, then we should like some brands until they try to dominate the narrative at our expense, or try to hijack a wholly irrelevant and inflated story for themselves. A story is only as good as how we relate to it. A potential user should not be treated merely as bait for a brand experience we are told we will enjoy. A brand is simply something we can choose to make a part of our day. Much can be done to improve realistic levels of expectation, and levels of disappointment, in the gap between brand managers for whom all brands have to make your entire day, and the realities of existence. We are no longer merely passive or reflexive in our brand behaviour, nor are we simply the sum of all the brands we use.

Why do gamers like gaming so much? Because they have more control. But this isn't about the pendulum swinging right to the far end of the 'Brand Me' arc. Brand Me is also missing the real point.

We only really exist in the context of other things. So do Brands.

Brands that are blatantly reconfigured only to worship me will also fail because they do not understand enough about the territories of engagement we set for our experiences with them.

Brand Me is overly focused, because we create many identities. Someone was wiser about today than he knew he could be: "I am large. I contain multitudes" – Walt Whitman. We do this identity creation literally through things like social network sites, but also with different sets of friends, relatives, colleagues, and strangers we encounter. In the olden days this was called hypocrisy or schizophrenia or deviousness, but it's just the way we are, and the way others construct their pictures of us. In a way it's the latest form of diffraction.

When you begin a new job, someone may say after a few months that they don't like your attitude about the company. Maybe they find you too critical of the status quo. Carry on doing the same thing and get a great result. Another person may then say what a fabulous person you are. What a great style you have. Attitude is a problem, style is a benefit. The only thing that changed was their perspective when confronted with new information.

Most brands can't or won't see this. They are still one-dimensional.

They try to find one thing they represent and then cling to it like a barnacle on a super tanker's bottom. The way we are is about richness not singularity. Like webs we are much more about unfettered connections than disconnected cells. Scared governments and companies don't like this, so they try and control our ability to connect and make connections. Brand owners don't want you to connect to others, only to them, first, and then maybe to others, through them. There was an early fashion when the web cranked up, and all kinds of brand managers started telling their communication agencies that they needed a full-blown web because they were going to be the portal to the world. Plenty of money was wasted on this pursuit. Then your brand had to be a social network 'friend'.

When was the last time you saw a car commercial where the car was full of stuff, like other brands, personal belongings, bits of you. It hardly ever happens. It doesn't happen because it's giving time, space, and control to others. It's monolithic, whereas you represent a whole set of 'yous', not just a narrow band of brands.

The old Rees Trout positioning statement summarised as "We – *put your brand name here* – stand out from the competition by virtue of our … " has a place but it is not the whole game anymore.

We stand out because you have decided we have what you demand and need now, electing us to perform that role, is a different perspective on the stand-out problem, even if it lacks elegance as a statement.

Some brands may have truly long-term viability, but most brands have a finite value, which can be extracted until it is exhausted, and then commoditised or left to pass away peacefully. Every so often, brands, like old mines, can be re-opened and exploited again, but this is not an option for every brand, nor would the product behind the brand be a choice for every future user.

Brands that continue to try to present themselves as diamonds when they are not will lose lustre and will only fool those who want to pretend they've got the real thing. Who's kidding whom?

The same applies to companies, and we referenced this through another source earlier. The story still stands through another lens. Of the 100 companies in *Forbes* magazine's first list of 1917, 60 were dead some 70 years later. Of the 39 survivors only 18 still numbered among the biggest 100 companies in 1987, and only two outperformed the stock market in that whole period. One of those was

Kodak, and look what happened to them. Sources of authority will continue to be challenged, in old and new ways. Somewhat unconsciously ironically, Rupert Murdoch said "Young people don't want to rely on a Godlike figure from above to tell them what's important. They want control over their own media, instead of being controlled by them." The same is true of frustrated brand managers.

Some paint the bleak picture of young people trapped in their bedrooms, not venturing outside, playing games. They still equate the scenario with loneliness. But this affluent person today is more connected to more people than ever.[4]

Young people often say they want fame and fortune. Whatever forms the desire takes, they see this as a right, and one that should come with no apparent effort. They deeply understand that celebrity can only belong to a few, so some of them go for something else that can transcend celebrity, and that's Respect. But even this takes on many forms, not all of them good. It's a matter of perspective again.

Respect is linked to reputation, good and bad, and comes these days with its own variable value and appraisal system. Nothing is isolated anymore.

Brands, then, can no longer be a single thing. A brand occupies a territory, and like a quantum particle, moves about its space with many possibilities and probabilities.

Depending on where you are as an observer, the brand's position looks different. It may seem to be in places that are closer to other territories. Those territories in turn have different influences, like gravitational pull, on the territory you are observing, and affect another observer's view. In fact, as we know from our elementary quantum physics, the very act of observance changes the position of things.

Look at it another way. A planet has an orbit. It may have an orbit around the Sun that takes it very close to the sun's heart at one end of the cycle, and very far away at the other. On its journey it comes close to the orbits of other planets, and they all have effects on each other. These influence how we perceive them, and how we interact with them.

In Brand Me World, this means different values can be ascribed to the same brand according to the viewer's, or user's perspective. We accord brand value points tacitly to brands that, in our opinion, show us more or less respect, or contribute to our definitions of value and reputation.

Brands that are adopted by groups as cohort symbols can create nightmares for brand owner observers, who see them being adopted "... by the wrong sort of people for the wrong reasons". Those connected to managing brands like Burberry, Doc Martens, Harley Davidson and plenty of others have gone through tough times until their view of the rebellion against the brand became normalised, or the rebellion became mythologised. So brands can find themselves in some pretty mixed company, which owners can celebrate or champ about.

Owners need to understand more about brand territories and orbits, tangential links, connections, and perceptions. Welcome to the multidimensional world of the modern person, who has always been like that, evolving in response to stimuli, but who has not been able to be observed like that in such rich terms before, nor often allowed to express themselves because of conditioning controls. Welcome also to the multidimensional world of probabilities for the brand.

Brands that are focused on users because they have high barriers to entry, like some luxury brands, have been able to watch more closely their more numerically limited audiences and respond to these kinds of understanding about behaviour in profitable ways.

In the late years of the first decade of this century many luxury brands were reporting revenue returns at up to 50% higher than already ambitious forecasts.[5] Brands continued to raise prices with no noticeable effect on sales until well after the credit crunch of 2008 had affected many other markets, which may have had a lot to do with the economics of scarcity they can enjoy. But also, they are building interactive formats with their clientele that enhance the observer's experience. For example, Jimmy Choo shoes create e-based intimate relationships with their customers without over-exposing, and so potentially diluting, their brand value. Jimmy-choo.com lets its shoppers view its shoes on avatars with the same dimensions as the shoppers. For these people, "I want to be special" has already morphed to "I am special", and then some to "I am a whole new/different world".

At micro and macro levels, things are apparently changing because we can see them more clearly. This has been the driver of The Scientific Method for hundreds of years, not forgetting that even where the finest scientific minds are, the ability to resist change remains profound. Why should it be any different for the finest minds in marketing?

It's tough, because more information can make it difficult to see the things behind the things. As the physicist Niels Bohr said, "If quantum physics hasn't profoundly shocked you, you haven't understood it yet".

This again is why science in the form of standard market research has often acted unwittingly as a misleading filter. Controlled psychology experiments, including focus groups, will systematically screen out habits and behaviour that affect real life, because they are designed to elicit responses to defined stimulus material, not the context in which that material will really exist.

The most successful brands are and will be the ones that understand how they can best help us to be the multiple selves we really are.

"I may not always know what's what, but I know what I'm going to get now", captures a piece of who it is we're trying to build a relationship with, and there are better ways than ever to enrich the value of that relationship.

Parents spend years trying to get their progeny not to be so selfish and demanding, only to have them walk into a world where that behaviour is condoned by myriads of brands, desperate to get their attention.

In a world where value is accorded to a brand by its user, based on the construct of their own world, in a market full of choices, lots of brands will still be deemed excellent, but for many of them that will come with a price, especially those that used to enjoy large volume sales. Formerly big brands may lose no 'collective values' – that is, the sum of the values all individuals ascribe to them, and in some cases will continue to gain values, but in many cases this will come with a diminution in volume sales. The challenge for brands with an increase in perceived values but a falling volume will be a critical challenge for companies whose cost structure has only supported maximising capacity or volume sales. Something's got to give. We might not have all the answers, but we've certainly got some proposals that will make the evolution less painful, and possibly more rewarding. But of course, as with all observation, it depends on how you are prepared to look at it.

Being able to enrich the role of brands, and their relevance, being able to help brand owners and users search deeper, further, wider, through personalised discovery channels, will enable people to understand more about rebellion and conformity, loyalty and rejection, functionality and desire, than ever. Surely this is better than accepting the simply given, or what is told to you by an expert who is reluctant or incapable of learning from the possibilities of improved levels of connectivity?

Perspective is vital for all communications. However straight and direct the beam you believe you are projecting with your message, there will be a prism or lens through which observers are diffracted from what you are trying to say, and which will affect their reception and interpretation of it. We can only see this relatively, and this is tempered by our experience, which plays a role in the construction of our views of and about the world. Psychologists call this our schemata. This is a condition of relativity, not unlike Einstein saying that the value of time depends on your point of observation. It all depends on where you're coming from, or where you're going to.

There are plenty of people who are handsomely rewarded for providing what we might call roles of refraction, trying to get your message received in as close a way as possible as the original intention. These can be researchers or planners, whose ideas and methodologies are expected, like lenses and mirrors, to help the investor in communication keep the gap between intention and perception close.

Unfortunately these additional observers can also sometimes be part of the process of diffraction, so messages can be distorted yet further.

All would be well if there was a purity of mediation and observation, but as we have noted already, this is like those early experiments into the nature of things quantum. The very act of observation can have a significant impact on how the thing observed is perceived. Things get more complicated the more mediators become involved, all of whose observations alter the way the message travels.

Each 'observer' has their own level of diffraction. Each argues for clarity, yet each has a particular perspective. The corrective lens for the myopic observer doesn't help the long-sighted see anything more clearly. So for all observers there are separate realities about brands and messages. There is the research reality, the media reality, the creative reality, and so on, all with their own contexts.

It is surprisingly difficult for people to see clearly through other lenses unless they share the same visual needs and their experiences are closely aligned. It's like trying to read the menu through someone else's glasses. So unless you are bold enough to say you can only imagine what it must be like to see things from another perspective, we tend to justify our own perspective as the real one. And no one is interested in paying for what they consider to be an unreal perspective.

Knowing this means many people in the chain strive hard to understand better which lens a client is looking through, and get as close to them as possible, so they think they are seeing through the looking glass together. Does this lead to bias? Almost surely.

Let us posit an experiment for a moment, just to see what effect it has on one particular perspective.

If a researcher or research company were paid for work from a trusted third party, holding funds in escrow, would objective reporting change?

In this experiment, companies forward money to a research fund that pays researchers for the job they do. This company briefs the researcher on the task in hand, so one form of potential bias, the client's, is replaced by another's, the trusted third parties. The researcher that tries to second guess the client's expectation is taking a big gamble, even though he knows, as we have suggested, that the expensive business of research is not generally used to kill owners' babies. It is regularly used to kill outsiders, like the ideas of communication agencies, through that other wonderful human survival and rejection process called the not-invented-here syndrome. Of course, you can argue that the trusted third party also has paymasters, and their own lenses in turn, but these are different lenses. Diffraction produces different perspectives. How would a cross analysis of objective reporting look?

Let's look a little further at these viewpoints. Some qualitative researchers would swear blind, an interesting notion in this context, that they are truly objective. In some ways they are, because they apply a unique level of diffraction to what they observe, through things like editing and précising the information they have collected in the field. The challenge for the viewers, or interpreters, is in trying to work out what form of objectivity they have been presented with. Getting to the truth, to the heart of the matter, turns out to be no easy thing. It is much more relative than they might have wanted to feel comfortable with.

In some markets this level of poking a stick in the bucket and swirling it around gets a better reception than in other places. If you happen to be in a French context with a strong tradition of intellectual analysis, a semiotician's point of view will be to offer that every person will always deconstruct a concept put before them according to their own unique experience, which means concepts can have many deconstructions and interpretations. A very different reaction might occur in another country context.

In some cases and places, where a client is known to the researcher, there can be a tendency for some to try and craft their own lens to have as little diffraction as possible from the client's. Sometimes it is only either the foolhardy, or the very brave, who bring bad news to demanding clients, and expect to get repeat business. It can be another costly effect of personal impacts on business that goes unrecorded in brand histories.

Other researchers would argue that they can be highly objective because they are not linked directly to the marketplace performance of what they are observing, so the pressure to succumb to favourable bias is discounted. Yet researchers too are often in pressured contexts, like in large companies dedicated to research, or tied to the corporation's objectives, and they are ultimately rewarded in this context, so there are always going to be parallel worlds or corporate demands and actions that have unwitting diffraction effects on behaviour and interpretation. The point here is not to challenge behaviour, so much as to reinforce the point about diffraction and its effect on interpretation and perception. The same data can be interpreted in different ways with very different consequences. The critical thing is to be aware of diffraction potential, and to learn how to manage it successfully.

The effects of diffraction travel wide. Those with overt creative roles can be equally affected. Many are lucky to believe they cannot be held directly to account for the fortunes of the brands and businesses they get connected to, and they can try and defend their actions as being objective, claiming they stand outside any circle of bias. But they too have their own diffractions.

If you don't believe this, see what happens when something goes wrong. Problems are always someone else's fault, and no, not all creative people are men. Problems exist in other worlds. "Don't you see what we've done, what we tried to do?" they all say. And did we indeed see it clearly? Sometimes, but often nothing was seen in advance at all.

This whole business is further distorted through the fact that few companies that are the originators and owners of brands will consistently test material, "knowing it to be bad". So whatever objectivity is brought to bear by the researcher, there has already been a textual or conceptual interpretation before the stimulus material has even been subjected to the researcher's microscope, macroscopic, or other observational device.

There are questions of presentation and stimulation that exist within the data itself, beyond any other form of bias, like perspectives borne out of the agendas of the participants in the brand and communication development process.

Acknowledging the possibility of diffraction can often influence its outcome. As we noted earlier, how many times have you ever heard people who have attended qualitative research groups say, "That's not what was said in my groups", when they hear a debrief being given by a researcher. It remains important to be conscious of the influences of diffraction, even if you subsequently choose to ignore the effects. It was a costly case as US and English space scientists stared blankly at each other when their prized $200 million space probe crashed ignominiously after a long journey, only to discover that one side had been working all along in imperial measures, and the other in metric. All was fine in macro terms – it was the micro details that got 'em.

The flavour or favour of particular media channels also takes its place in the diffraction process. For example, how can you sit in a communications company, claiming to be media neutral? Some of those companies issued contracts to senior creative people saying they only had to work on TV commercials. Dominant media channels attract supporting models and rationales. Often lucrative tools are developed to quantify the effectiveness of a particular media channel and its content, which then extend to being apparently predictive. They also have beautiful ways, for an additional analysis fee, of presenting to you in glorious microscopic detail why things didn't quite go the way that was anticipated. Since there are so many variables to play with this can be another fertile ground. Effectiveness drives advocacy.

So, no-one finds a replacement for the 30-second TV commercial.

So what? It may continue to have a role, just like press advertising does, and radio, and on-line, and all the other media. But while television's place as an effective medium may continue to be tested and advocated, its role as the centrepiece of a range of relevant communications for many brands or businesses is past its sell-by date for many, and should be.

Companies in the communications business are always talking about how they are in the ideas business these days. Media neutral might be a client cry, but most folks out there are still thinking in ways driven by media channels. Look at the wave of digital agencies that were snapped up by mature communications companies. Next come the social network agencies. Very few people are able to generate and present ideas that can be understood and sold outside the context of a medium, and just as few people are able to get it on the receiving end either. Even if an idea can be beautifully expressed, it takes a different kind of skill, or perspective, to be able to translate that into graspable forms. Most people are the same. They don't want abstractions. 'Show me' is what they want. "I'll know it when I see it" is a fact of life. We said that about the way many brand users are today – why should it be different in the office?

This raises important questions about where good ideas might come from, and then what they might look like, sound like, and feel like, as we move forward through diffractions. Judging whether they have value and what that is, remains a critical issue and challenge.

There's also another dilemma here. Many of the issues in this chapter, until the very end, have had less to do with brand users than with brand management teams and all their service providers. How are they going to fit in with all this, you might ask? Once again, turn that around. How are we going to fit in with them? If there's no room, or no spark, there's no point. For many over-researched professional respondents, they'll take the money, but the point these days is, as the comedienne Catherine Tate once got famous for saying, "Am I bothered? Am I really, really bothered?"

We only really exist in the context of other things. So do Brands.

Brands, then, can no longer be a single thing. A brand occupies a territory, and like a quantum particle, moves about its space with many possibilities and probabilities.

The most successful brands are and will be the ones that understand how they can best help us to be the multiple selves we really are.

6. Strategy. Are We Asking the Wrong Questions?

In Part 2 of this book, we are going to propose a fresh way of looking at brands and how to get more value from them that is more relevant and practical than many other models. It is also simpler than fashionable. But before we do that, there is still work to be done on other core issues. Coming out of our analyses so far, we say there is not simply one idealistic pure-point or pedestal for a successful brand to be located at. A brand does not have to involve traditional and established criteria to be judged as successful. Brand owners, in working to create better products and services, can look to more realistic ways to determine the nature of their relationships with users, and how to talk to them.

Profound emotional connection with many brands is simply wishful thinking, and this is an indulgence that should be transferred into more relevant and productive forms of functionality or connecting with people. To establish the context for bringing our model to life, we still need to look at one more vital area - and this is about the kinds of questions we ask ourselves in thinking about the development of competitive and compelling strategies. Even if you choose not to use the perspective on brands that we develop, what we take up here can still lead to greater efficiencies in building profitable brand owner-manager-user relationships. We begin by first re-visiting current common best practice, and ask ourselves the challenging thing – are we simply asking the wrong questions?

Generally speaking, and under whichever proprietary name the communications company and/or client choose to describe them, the tendency is to look in strategy creation at variations in these kinds of key questions:

- Who is the target audience?

- What is the key user/customer insight?

- What does the brand offer as a benefit?

- Why should the target audience believe the offer?

- What is the personality, and/or what are the values of the brand?

- What is the brand's competitive differentiation?

Let's look at each of these in turn.

Target Audience

All too often, it is still unfortunately the case that this is set out in terms of old-fashioned demographics and psychographics, and as we have shown, this is of decreasing relevance in today's world. Understandably, client researchers and other marketing folk set great store on really trying to understand 'user attitudes to their category and brand', and faithfully reproduce whatever data they can muster, in the brief that goes to the communications producers. This is useful. But increasingly it is necessary to go much further than this. When do we ever see, for example, the fact about how long it takes a customer to select a brand of toothpaste? On average it takes 11 seconds. Yet surely this point is important. Indeed it constitutes one of Procter & Gamble's 'Two Moments of Truth' in terms of customer interaction with products at point of sale. How often are you really honest about how customers feel about competitive brands, especially if you are honest enough to admit to yourself that they might indeed be more attractive than your own brand? And how often do we ask what users really want to know, as opposed to what we want to tell them?

Equally importantly, there is often no mention in the communications brief of how your customers feel about communications in the category, not to mention in the world at large, nor how they interact with media channels generally – and clearly, this is of huge and growing importance. Currently many of the established larger communication conglomerates remain mesmerised by all things socially networked – but these are just the next form of delivery channel, which need to be set into the context of life today. There'll be something else along soon, which will also join the menu of possibilities.

Key Insight

This topic has probably received more attention than most other aspects of the communication briefing process over the last fifteen years. Planners and researchers have put enormous effort into finding what they have defined as ever more interesting user insights, believing these to be critical to both innovation and communication development. This has been driven by clients demanding them. They are marketing weapons of mass incremental business. So they must exist. Research methodologies have been developed to uncover the inner workings of people's subconscious minds, to reveal deeply meaningful insights, which might stimulate ever more fanciful creative ideas. Imagine the researcher who arrives to debrief a communications company on a range of creative ideas for a draught beer, and who announces to his enthralled audience that he has asked his unfortunate respondents to create clay models to show how they feel about the brand. It makes great theatre, and is indeed very entertaining, but is this what the respondents really feel? Or are they just going along with this to get a long four hours and often frankly quite tedious experience out of the way?

We have actually heard women in qualitative research groups saying to each other in the refreshment periods, "Well Joyce, I think we're here for the travel stuff today. Didn't see you at the biscuits session last week, are you OK?" Whatever recruiters may say, we know there is a band of professional respondents out there. It's a bit like the first time you discovered that perhaps Jerry Springer's audiences were not all quite plain folks off the street. Let us not be cynical and posit that groups may be untainted. Do insights really help? We are of the view that the conventional take on user insights is not always as helpful as it might appear. Firstly, insights are almost always generic to a category – they are rarely specific to brands. This being the case, they are very difficult for a brand to own.

"Ah, yes", you might say, "but what about Kit Kat's *Take a Break*, or Heineken's *Refreshes the parts*?"

Our response would be that these are both established brands which consistently said virtually the same thing for over forty years so that they effectively owned the category generic. They almost got the star prize of becoming category-defining nouns and verbs, like our old friends Hoover and Biro. But try doing it today, and you'll find it's a lot more difficult. It happens, like with 'to google', but it's quite rare. If you choose to buy a communication idea based on a user insight, and manifest it in a fairly traditional way, like in mass/individualised media, the chances are that any pre-test will tell you that you have a branding problem – i.e. people may or may not be able to recall the communication, but they have no idea who it's from. And why should they – because the most interesting thing about the communication is not what the brand offers, but how the user behaves in any given category? Even if you manage to avoid this issue, just because an insight is true, does not mean that the insight will necessarily motivate people. Imagine a scenario that took place around ten years ago. A leading manufacturer of detergents, worn down by countless user groups telling them that the most powerful 'demonstration of clean' was getting into bed when the sheets had just been changed, instructed their agency to develop a commercial to capitalise on this apparently universal user insight. So confident were all involved parties of its success, that the pre-test was not conducted as an animatic (a rough testing version of a film) - but on the finished film. It achieved one of the worst ever recorded scores on this particular pre-test methodology in the UK. Why? Because, as an insight, it was true, but not surprising or different – so no one felt they needed to pay it any attention.

On the other hand, insights about user attitudes to communication can have powerful effects. In the late 1990's, Unilever decided to steal a march on Procter & Gamble and bring a format innovation to market – detergent tablets – under the Persil brand. Anyone who has worked in this category will know that most UK, and in fact any developed market users, have a fairly well defined "hate" relationship with detergent advertising. This began as long ago as the 1960s when the Advertising Standards Authority legislated to restrict the number of detergent commercials on ITV to one per hour, so numerous were complaints about them. More recently, detergent ads are roundly criticised for

a)   being economical with the truth – e.g. removes chocolate stains at 40 degrees. Any Mum will attest in a group that this is not the case, and

b)   stereotyping women's roles – as late as 1996 there were still numerous examples on our TV screens of women taking enormous interest in the removal of a stain from a football shirt so that the son and heir could go out and do the family proud.

So Unilever took a very brave decision – not to focus on a user insight about the category to develop the communication to support the launch of their new product but to make the insight about women's attitudes to communication in the category central to the brief. The resulting launch programme broke all category conventions, and got delirious reviews in research. "At last" said Mums all around the country, "A brand that really does understand how I feel about doing the laundry". The business results weren't bad either at that time. Persil regained brand leadership from Ariel, taking it to a healthy share of the UK market, proof positive that communication insights might just be quite important, sometimes.

Of course, that market place is a well-established brand manufacturer theatre of engagement, and like the Hundred Years War, is likely to witness many further battles yet. This was just one old war story, but one with a telling message and implications. Fighting on the brand user's terms, having got to understand them, may not only be more cost effective than working on average product delivery improvements, but it may help maintain product sales while the savings are invested into leaps, not increments, in product delivery. In the winner's enclosure, the spoils go to the one who does both of these.

What the Brand offers as a Benefit

It has become common practice to define at least two benefits for many brands, one functional and one emotional. In some instances this continues to make good sense, for example, with highly-specified aspirational goods. But we would caution about the importance of deciding the balance of which is the more potent driving factor in user choice, whether this dualism always makes sense in the world in which we live today, and just how many brands this approach can really apply to.

A brand like Google may be highly technical, but not necessarily involved in a particularly emotional relationship with most of its users. It is important that a brand is transparent and reliable, and these attributes should be fundamental requirements of all successful brands today. What is interesting, in our view, is that Google does not seek a 'unique emotional benefit'. But no one could argue that it is not a very powerful brand, or should we put it another way? A lot of people would say Google is a brand, and then try and make it fit their predetermined, high-emotional element model. Does this say something about brands, or about models? Al Qaeda is a well-known entity, and certainly as well-known as many brands. What kind of brand is it? It depends on the perspective of the observer. And even Google has been faced with issues over transparency and motive.

In other instances, the argument goes, we need an emotional benefit to avoid being generic / at the mercy of own labels etc., etc. But we would argue that for many brands, if you do not have demonstrable functionality, you are not long for this world anyway. As we have shown above, users are increasingly cynical, and will eventually turn away from brands that do not operate in both an ethical and transparent way, unless they are waging a jihad. Inventing a higher order emotional benefit to distract people from the performance reality is likely to be seen for what it is – an avoidance, or worse, an evasive, strategy. It is much better, in our view, to simplify this, and not force the creation of a higher order emotional benefit for brands that do not sit high-up in a person's "I really want to be in love with this" list.

Why should a user believe the offer? If the brand is claiming a predominantly rational contribution to your life, a 'reason to believe' can be useful, if it is compelling and credible – but not just for the sake of it. 'New Improved' is better than a quasi-scientific explanation of why 'x' molecule does 'y' to your hair follicle. Unless you can prove this in a convincing fashion, today's users are very unlikely to be taken in by this kind of approach, and certainly not after a failed product trial on themselves. Because they've heard it all before. For the last forty years marketing people and their communication providers have invested huge amounts of money to 'prove' the latest product advances deliver, and all too often they haven't been true, or, at the very least, were significant over-claims. And users today know that. They heard the claim and bought the product, only to discover that it didn't meet the expectation created by the communication. So they stop buying it, and make a mental note to be a little less gullible next time. When this has been repeated hundreds or thousands of times across categories and products, a kind of evolutionary process of protection from gullibility kicks in, and becomes a part of that next generation's zeitgeist. We have taught them to be wary – thus our plea for transparency. If you don't have a convincing point of difference, don't waste time and money trying to make one up – the odds are it won't be believed anyway. Consider using the marketing support differently. It's time to treat users as they deserve – not as mindless receivers of data designed to drive them to one brand versus another, but as intelligent de-coders of all the ways in which we are trying to connect with them. We still have choices.

Personality or Values of the Brand

This is a complex area. If, as has been noted earlier, and as is often described in best practice text books, brands exist predominantly as sets of facts and impressions in the minds of their users – how can they have one single defined personality? It may have made sense initially in the early days of marketing. When there was less concern or even knowledge about the complexity of users' interactions with brands, for owners struggling to find how to present their brands in a way that differentiated them from competition it may have been valuable to be the brand with a clear and one-dimensional personality, but increasingly we believe we need to review this 'given'. Let's revisit what we touched upon earlier.

What still happens all too often is that brand owners and their respective communication providers negotiate an acceptable list of words to describe their brand's personality. As we also observed, this is rarely less than five words that may include such diverse yet ubiquitous words as 'accessible, friendly, confident, authoritative, fun', or it may stretch to as many as ten or twelve words. These are so often generic they are redundant. They also don't stand up to the test of opposing value i.e. would you ever describe your brand as 'inaccessible, unfriendly, diffident, ignorant, and dull'? Yet again we see brands trying to own one sweet spot that is overcrowded and not liberating. It's like the tired line that comes at the end of the "what we're here to do" part of brainstorming sessions – "And most importantly, we're going to have fun".

Sometimes you witness clever catch-all phrases like 'the spirit and inspiration of the market place', which encompasses all the inputs of its creators, but is meaningless to the uninitiated majority. What does it mean? It means lots of different things, to lots of different people –

again depending on your perspective. Your favourite is the next one's least favourite. So if you have to insist on having a personality for your brand, try and make it special, a memorably rich character. It's not as easy as you might think, and memorable characters often polarise views further. Are you really lost without the character or personality descriptor?

Competitive Differentiation

This is a critical question – and another one that it is most difficult to be honest about because, let's face it, sometimes our brand isn't really better than the competition, it's just different. Throw the user's perspective in as well and your perceived superior product may also not be recognised as such because of other distortions and diffractions the user has become accustomed to viewing your brand through. That is the key point. We have, ultimately, to accept that for a lot of established brands the practical position we should take on this is how we are viewed in a competitive context from real life people's points of view, with all the natural shifts in perception they apply. It may be frustrating, but it's the way things are.

Do what you can with what you've got. Sometimes you will be able to improve, even radically, what you have, or what you represent, and you must approach that honestly. It is simply dumb to keep thinking you are the best if all that adds up to is the volume of your protestations about it. Ultimate judgement in the market place is not in your gift. It often doesn't matter what happens in a laboratory. The users need to be able to see, hear, taste, smell, or feel some point of difference for themselves, or it doesn't count. This does not mean, by the way, the end of product demonstrations - there are some great examples around – like our fondness for Ronseal's, "Does exactly what it says on the tin", but what it does mean is that we should be a lot more direct about the reality of our product's performance and stop kidding ourselves that we've got Superman when what we're really talking about is Couch Potato.....

New Perspectives on Strategy

We think it is time to open up the debate by re-framing the kinds of core questions we want strategies to address, and our responses to them. What questions might be both more helpful, and relevant, as we move forward? In terms of framing a new approach to strategy creation, we have developed the following five key challenges that need to be addressed robustly and honestly.

1. What does this brand do best?

First of all, you need to know what kind of brand you have. This could have an emotional element, a functional element, empathetic, connective, interactive or other elements and combinations. In Part Two we look at how this process of definition can be simplified to avoid redundancies or false perspectives. It is not about creating an endless list of superlatives. It's about deciding what the brand does best for people today, and what it could do best in the near future. It's about being honest, clear, transparent, and focused. It is not about making up superfluous benefits for categories and brands where users don't need them.

So things like:

- Drink X brand of coffee and it will inspire you to be a more creative person

- Use Y bank and it will set you free

- Use Z hand-cream or your husband will reject you (because you have wrinkly hands)
  …..should all be avoided.

2. What is the most meaningful way to present your brand?

This is a more practical way of satisfying questions about the pre-occupations with brand personality. The current practice of developing an often over-long list of adjectives makes less and less sense – for anyone. Users, scientists, marketers and creative people all have differing perspectives – so a catch-all list may well satisfy everyone's different perspectives, differently, but it is unlikely to guide anything in a meaningful way, one that will give direction for action and execution. People tend to choose one or two words from the list, execute something around that, and then call it interpretation. This leads to disaffection. It is another piece of diffraction. Our proposal is that brand owners and managers should define the style of presentation they want for a brand – and agree this with key stakeholders. This should be borne out of an analysis of data that can usefully be assembled to help refine the thinking. The asset of the presentation style should be firmly the intellectual property of the brand owner.

For example, Virgin tries consistently to own wittiness in its communications. It's always trying to challenge incumbents. It's always trying to say, "Hey, we know what life is like, just like you do, so let's get on with it together. We're just here to try and make the journey a bit easier and more enjoyable." Yes, even on Virgin Trains. Now, one could argue that the style has been crafted to reflect the projected personality of its owner. But Mr Branson (Sir Richard) has reduced his presence as the overt manifestation of the brand, so that when he gives up, or throws off the mortal coil, the brand can maintain its style of presentation, in the spirit of its founder, without his actual presence. Style of presentation is more about form than simply a function of personality. The style of presentation is often what users engage with, so brand personality is already sublimated within this. We have already said that in any case brands have multiple variations of personality driven by the perspectives of users. A good style of presentation allows the user to have enough space to create their own relationship with the brand without having to buy into an overly-defined personality. It is more important to define the way you present the brand than to perform Dickensian feats of characterisation about your brand's alleged personality – users will do that for you.

3. Why should the user pay attention to the brand, on and in their terms?

In answering this challenge it is essential to ask how the brand is or will be seen in the context of users' lives, and capture how users will see it as being different.

What does this brand really provide people with in the context of their lives? This represents a fundamental shift from the way many brands are managed today. Brand managers are used to telling people what a brand offers from their perspective. Our view is that this is an increasingly irrelevant model. In a lot of cases, it should be the other way around. Many people with the word 'creative' in their job descriptor describe much of Procter & Gamble's communications as formulaic and dull, unless they are the respected senior creative players on the business of course. Yet what the company does unquestionably well is to place their brands into wholly credible situations in everyday life. Much of the immensely effective Tide detergent advertising globally is really based on that most powerful marketing tool - word of mouth, on TV. It is given fame by the use of credible local celebrities who invite women to see for themselves which brand washes whiter etc. It may not be glamorous, but it is very persuasive and the brand actually delivers functionally.

The key challenge here is to define what the user's principles and values are that drive your business. These can help you get away from the whirlpools of debates about brand personalities which can rarely be translated into useful and productive messages beyond internal communications documents.

4. What results do you expect from brand support activity?

How will you know whether your activity has been successful? There are lots of questions that can be asked here, in lots of different ways. But one of the most common misapprehensions occurs when the assumption is made that if you change an attitude which you believe is hindering your performance in a market, this will automatically translate into measurable improved market performance. Sadly, and all too often, this is not the case. We return again briefly to our fascination with detergents, primarily because they furnish such excellent examples for us. Take the manufacturer who believed that his brand was losing share to a new competitive brand because it lagged behind its new rival in user perceptions about the delivery of functional whiteness. He challenged his advertising agency to come up with advertising that "single-mindedly communicated" his brand's "whiteness credentials". They did. Six months later, his brand's whiteness scores were improving – but his sales were not. Maybe this was because whiteness is no longer a real discriminator for a detergent – after all, many brands claim to wash whiter. Or maybe it was because the rival was building more authentic credentials, and took the trouble to look at itself through the eyes of its customers, and reflect that back through communications that contextualised the brand realistically in the users' lives.

Or take the case of a Marketing Director charged with improving the fortunes of a very big old food brand. He assiduously followed all the golden rules of marketing, was extremely focused, disciplined and consistent in his approach to communications, and after two years was rewarded with dramatically improved brand image and attitudes according to all his market research data. "Why, when we've done everything by the book" he asked one of us, "don't I see any improvement in my sales performance?" This is one of the key questions we laid down at the beginning of the book.

His research experts talked about time lag. Maybe. More likely is the explanation that his product range was of decreasing relevance to his customer base. Women's attitudes to food and food preparation have and are changing at a phenomenal rate across Europe, and his product range was of decreasing interest. Perhaps if the company had had the courage to really look at what they delivered through the eyes of its customers, and not its shareholders and stakeholders the issue, and what to do about it, could have been addressed earlier. So studies that purport to look at attitudes to brands in isolation, or just in the context of the product category that they operate in, versus the user category or space they exist in, may no longer be that helpful – it is vital to think more carefully about what you really expect to happen as a result of what you're doing.

We also believe that research agencies should think further about how they are evaluating communications in light of what we are describing as real versus hoped-for behaviour in marketplaces. It's all too easy still to focus on old established broadcast media. It has the most developed research methodologies to measure its performance, and it remains one of the single most expensive items in the communications mix in many markets. But this form of communication is increasingly ignored by a growing number of users – either actively by channel switching or ad skipping in the case of TV, or passively - it is there only as background noise to other displacement activities, and in other forms it is also simply a skip-over process. By and large, most TV pre-testing methodology in the UK is pretty fair in its own controlled context. You get to see an ad two or three times and then you are asked which brand it's for, what it's saying, whether you like it or not, whether it might make you want to try the brand, and so on. Some companies have also gone as far as to differentiate between ads whose intent is to drive short-term sales, and ads whose purpose is to develop brand imagery. And it all seems reasonable enough. There is plenty to read about in the literature of the media on these types of topics.

Reality bites. Most people do not watch advertising closely or pay that much attention to it at all in their actual lives. The assumption on which pre-tests are often based is false – people do not actively consume advertising anymore, so even if you get a great score, it doesn't necessarily mean that anyone will actually notice your communication – much less act on it.

Time for a re-think we think. Media companies are thinking about this – which is good news as it needs urgent attention.

5. How will you have prepared for the truly unexpected?

It's very easy, when you're working in a particular culture, or organisation, to become myopic, and always consider what others might do through the lens of your own particular world. This can often lead to the view that "the competition would never do that, because we wouldn't," and this can limit potential for innovation as well as leaving you vulnerable to unexpected attacks. To illustrate the point – when running a workshop to develop a new range of food products, we conducted an initial exercise in which we asked all the participants to imagine that Richard Branson had just bought the brand, and asked them to say what they thought he would do to modernise it. Immediately, lots of great ideas came up – partnership with other Virgin products, demos, take-away party packs and so on. When we got back to client base the ideas were much more constrained, conforming to accepted corporate wisdom within that company's operating culture – sponsoring a long lasting barbecue to try for a world record was one of the more ambitious ones.

From another perspective, the inability to imagine scenarios through different lenses can pose a real threat to business success. We opened the book with this observation. One former client, when posed with a big competitive entry into his market, organised a workshop to try to imagine what that competitor might do. The worst case scenario had the competitor cutting the price of his brand by 20%-25%. Reality was much worse. The competitor dropped his price point by 50% - seriously damaging the client's business in the short term. It was beyond everyone's worst nightmare – because it was something that the client's culture would never have considered.

So in our view it's important to think "What If?" with different lenses. Come up with your worst nightmare, and then make it worse – for all aspects of brand development.

It helps to enlist some non-partisan participants. Sometimes people who don't know the category, or are not members of the company, can shed realistic light on probabilities and possibilities. This almost always produces different perspectives. And in order to think about your own potential response to change initiated by others you don't know, that's exactly what you need. Return now from the challenges to the chapter title, "Strategy. Are We Asking the Wrong Questions?" this is also clearly about perspective. It needs discipline, knowledge, intelligence, inspiration, insight, and intuition[1]. As perspective, strategy raises intriguing questions about intention and behaviour in a collective context, both by users, and by the corporations that serve them.

"In great companies, strategy becomes a cause, because strategy is about being different".

Creating the best context for strategy development

In a competitive world, strategy, like other forms of creativity, needs to create new perspectives as well as new creations. People, especially those in research and planning functions, often believe that the more information there is, the more accurate consequent decisions will be. We would like to repeat that empirical evidence often does not support this belief.

Instead, more information merely seems to increase the confidence that we are right without necessarily improving the accuracy of our decisions. This is not to say we don't need information, but it is to say that we need to know more about the kinds of information we collect, and its accuracy. This is absolutely about quality, not quantity. More and more data collection may reveal more trees – but it often also prevents you from seeing the bigger picture i.e. the forest itself. The best strategizing depends on creating a rich and complex web of conversations that cuts across previously isolated pockets of knowledge and creates new and unexpected combinations of insight. The manager who has built or inherited a 'rigid' organisation may not be able to come up with an idea which nobody in the company has ever thought of before, but his most significant contribution may be that he can see relationships, and potential through those, which no-one else has seen. This is tacit or intuitive strategic ability.

We like familiar tales and stories, but we also need to be aware of the narrative fallacy [2]. This is about our all too human limitation in not being able to look at sequences of events or facts without "weaving an explanation into them, or forcing an arrow of relationship upon them. Explanations help things make more sense". We need to simplify things, but we also need to be aware of the dangers of assuming connections and logic where none exist in reality. Reality doesn't always model itself on case studies. How is insight to come from debates about products no-one has ever touched, for customers no-one has ever met?[3]

---

1. What does this brand do best?
2. What is the most meaningful way to present your brand?
3. Why should the user pay attention to the brand, on and in their terms?
4. What results do you expect from brand support activity?
5. How will you have prepared for the truly unexpected?

---

7. As a Client – Who Can I Turn to for the Best Advice?

Many people want to be close to those who have the gift of bestowing rewards and of showing that by taking a firm grasp of leading a team to deliver the wishes of the Bestower, they are also worthy followers and potential leaders.

Yet again, perspective distorts clarity in understanding how leadership objectives are formed, and where they might take you to. To get the ball rolling, revisit online the timeless text from a couple of baseball watchers, otherwise remembered as Abbott and Costello, with their famous commentary, *Who's On First?*

When you go to seminars, conferences, brainstorms, or any other of these kinds of meetings, they usually include sessions that attempt to define who does what, best. In marketing communications, for years and years there was a hierarchy like the medieval 'Great Chain of Being'. For continuing entertainment's sake, things were like the famous Frost Report TV sketch of the '60s. There was the tall John Cleese standing in his pin-striped suit with his bowler atop his head. Next to him was the rotund Ronnie Barker in his tweeds and middle-ranking civil servant attire, and then came little Ronnie Corbett in his mac and flat cap. Cleese said he looked down on every one because he was upper class. Barker said he looked up to the upper class and down to the lower class. Corbett paused and said "I know my place". Guess which kind of company played the Cleese role? The Advertising Agency of course. The Mad Men.

Then things got complicated. All kinds of service companies started to decide that they too could own strategy, and although many of them still had significant revenues from their original core competencies, they started to offer competing services in other disciplines, whether that was media or execution services. And guess what? What solutions looked like was different according to the founding perspective of the generating agent.

There were occasionally other threats, like when agencies thought that big consulting companies were going to eat their lunch. The big consulting companies quickly worked out that their revenue usually came from the higher levels of brand owning companies, where compensation was equally at other strata. But communications companies continued to look on in envy at the big boys, and almost anyone now offers services on top of their core business that try to push them onto clients' strategic high ground. That way attention and bigger budgets lie. Of course, everyone also has a reason why their particular perspective should be sought out, listened to, and paid for.

Today's communication agencies continue to think they own the right to being their client's right hand, while often under-investing in their ability to provide proprietary insights. They have shed expertise to focus on untrammelled ideas. This is purity, like faith without any need for supporting evidence. Disbelievers continue to be mocked, attacked, or undermined.

"How can you get the advice you need from a direct marketing agency?" used to come the sneering line from companies that believed themselves to be on a higher plain. Now successful direct marketing, digital, and design companies and agencies have morphed and evolved and use the same arguments the old advertising agencies practised.

"Listen to us. We go through the same processes as those other guys, to get to know you, your brands, and your customers. But our processes are deeper, faster, more cost effective. Let us have a go first."

Clients get confused once they've got over being grateful.

However tightly you think you have written the brief of a tender, the very starting point of the respondent's action will affect their perspective, and the results you see. Design companies will produce brilliant thoughts that can be turned into advertising, through-the-line companies can provide insights that will elicit new levels of enthusiasm from product engineers, branded content creators may come up with ideas for videos or games or movies.

As a client you have a richness of responses. So where's the catch? Well, there's more than one catch.

All of the above eventually make presentations to show how things would be better in the future if the presenters had a little more control of the processes and the hierarchies, from strategy to brand expression to execution. "If only we were a little closer to the centre, what a better job we could do", they all propose.

The cautious client says, "I might give you a chance". He doesn't want to stop you producing free ideas. "How do I know I'm getting a better solution? Who do I turn to, because I sure as hell don't have the time or money to give everyone a chance? All I know is I can't keep buying the old stuff in the old way, because it's not working for my business any more. What should a solution look like for my business?"

"Trust us", say the solution providers, and lo and behold they come up with solutions that are principally driven by and derived from their revenue comfort zones, often unwittingly. And are you really surprised?

We will come back to this issue, and how to manage it, later. Suffice to say this is, in our view, getting in the way of clients effectively managing their brands.

Here's an interesting scenario that brings to light a different kind of problem.

A trusted planner is asked to attend more meetings, to become a key partner to a client, an essential adjunct. The planner's own company resents the time it's paying the asset while the planner is away from the office. The planner becomes more productive from the client's perspective, but less popular from the communication's company perspective. The planner's thinking is respected by the client, but it cannot easily be turned into the products the agency supplies. Where does that leave the planner, and the client relationship?

The planner had built what the client believed to be a relevant and helpful bridge, but the planner's employers didn`t like it. It was not a happy outcome for any of the parties.

Ideas then get withdrawn because there aren't enough brave agents or representatives of change to keep pushing, and in some cases not enough really brave clients either. Alternatively, new ideas are repressed because they don't lead to immediate revenue generation for the incumbent, and there is often little in compensation agreements to encourage the sharing of revenue for the greater good of a collective enterprise, or group.

Interestingly, people with the word 'creative' in their role descriptions also often find the new and emerging worlds difficult too. For years, they have been able to call the shots as the prime generators of ideas, and as such have created their own comfort zones:

- "I don't read briefs"

- "I don't do client meetings"

- "You can't say two things, only one"

- "Don't argue. You see all those awards?

- "My idea is the one we're going to present"

It's all a bit rich given that it's actually very difficult to prove the value of their component contribution to a brand's success, despite noble pieces of post-rationalisation like the established Institute of Practitioners in Advertising's Advertising Effectiveness Awards. Two of the key contributors to this book have had six papers awarded in these awards over 20 years, including the Grand Prix, so we know something about post-rationalisation and the challenges of the burden of proof.

How many people's perspective might be shifted if they subjected themselves to this simple but worthy test?

"Would you believe this proposition yourself, and act upon it?"

As we've said earlier, the usual exit-line is along the lines of, "But I'm not the target audience". It's easy to hide behind waffle or diversionary tactics in support of weak ideas.

In our experience consistently great creative people work harder, think deeper, and know their client's business better than most, while still being original, iconoclastic, relevant, engaging, and memorable. But there aren't too many of those in a box. Of course there's a role for good creative people to turn ideas into useable tangible materials, but where can they be found? Not always where you think, and not always in communication agencies. Great storytellers are often brand originators, inventors, and entrepreneurs.

Brands, through the inspiration of their founders, have often been described as being able to tell you clearly and interestingly who they are and what they stand for. But are these statements relevant for most brands today? No. We are left with some interesting challenges. If this really is the case, let's note some of them:

- What motivating brand values can be espoused today?

- If you are not the brand originator, how do you generate stimulating ideas?

- Where do you get them from?
- How do you generate ideas independently from media channels?
- How do you manage the effects of mediation?
- Who controls all this?

Organisation and structure influences brand destiny, just as ego and subjectivity does. There is a fascinating interplay which brands reflect at deeper levels of analysis.

What happens when you separate leading from managing? In many organisations too many people want to lead. Too many keep solving new problems without having to face the consequences of solving the previous ones. Communications companies are now full of people who have been rocketed into leadership positions with little management experience. What is the effect of putting a leader into a place with no appreciation of its history, and no sense of its culture? What is the effect of imposing a detached outsider on committed insiders? "Sure, a new broom sweeps clean, but...they are often more experienced at sweeping out experienced people than sweeping in new ideas." The result of this leads to leadership being coveted as a means to get ahead personally rather than make an organisation a better place. Ironically, this can result in a style of management that is actually devoid of leadership[1]. Brands in this kind of environment can become victims of the so-called leaders, or are used or sublimated to the end-game desires of the individual in pursuit of the Main Job.

"The creation of strategy requires invention more than calculation, from connected minds that are able to see a different future". Put the average communication company team together and this will be significantly hindered because, "I think it fair to say that these people want to create the team and lead it to some glory, as opposed to being a member of a team that's being driven by somebody else"[2]. This is a lot to do with the emergence of self-centred individuality. It's the mediated issue again. Balance in a team is critical, but only if the players can respect other styles.

Business and the press got caught up in this form of hero worship habit in the 1990s and early 2000s, which exacerbated this kind of problem by eulogising lone leaders as saviours. Individual leaders were put on pedestals, at the expense of others, often giving the impression to outsiders that the "Leader somehow did everything that mattered entirely themselves". The revolving door of this talent had little bearing on the company's actual performance. These people arrived and made promises with other people's money. If stocks rose they cashed in. If stocks fell they left with golden parachutes sanctioned by cowardly or partisan compensation committees, all legally compliant. In this world, outsiders remained favoured. Anyone who knew the business inside out was suspect, so new teams were always in demand, and heroes were also those who were demanded the most. "The very characteristics that get people into senior positions undermine their performance once there – they are too smart, too fast, too confident, self-serving, and disconnected. Many of the white knights of heroic management turn out to be the black knights of corporate performance"[3]. Management needs to be in different places. For example, seeing yourself at the centre of an organisation, rather than on top of it, changes perceptions about the managerial world. In a web-connected environment management needs to be everywhere, which suggests that management has to be potentially everyone. So in a network, authority for making decisions and developing strategic initiatives has to be distributed, so that responsibility can flow to those best able to deal with the issues at hand. Control gives way to collaboration, command and control gives way to connecting and contributing. That means managers have to be inside networks, not just tangential to them, intent on leading the team. Now, try to change that in a context which has seen the glorification of self-interest grow faster than at any time since the 1920s, like in the US for example. Greed was raised to some sort of high calling, and CEOs and others with leadership titles were regarded as if they alone created economic performance. How can discussion about a brand's value be taken seriously in this context? It can only happen if deference is given to the advantage of distributed intelligence, not totemic hero worship. It's about context and perspective again. The creative group that supports the leader demanding the design of faster horse drawn carriages is immune to the Wright Brothers. Truly successful communication companies should fight to dismiss all irrelevancies that prevent them from being in the business of making worthwhile connections.

"It is not revolution or reorganisation we need so much as re-conception. We need to get our heads around what we do, as compared with what we claim to do. Change will come from the rise of competing alternatives." [4]

For many, alternatives come at a welcomingly slow rate, leaving swathes of folk to retire successfully after career-long resistance to change.

This brings us back to the question of who can you turn to. How you feel about that depends on who you are and what perspectives you have about idea generation. We invited you into this chapter where we posed the question but didn't totally answer it. To finalise the answer we felt we needed to get through more observations, so this has been a demonstration of the effects of diffraction on perception.

The rest of the book seeks to provide the practical propositions to tackle these critical issues.

Many people want to be close to those who have the gift of bestowing rewards, and of showing that by taking a firm grasp of leading a team to deliver the wishes of the Bestower, they are also worthy followers and potential leaders.

"Would you believe this proposition yourself, and act upon it?"

If the subjectivity of people is a key driver of strategy, rather than it being a highly objective process, what should we do about it?

Part Two

Brands and Reality – How to Be Simply the Best

8. Stickiness and the Power of Simplification

Where do we begin to think about how to find a more effective way forward in terms of shaping and managing brands?

The first step is to acknowledge again where we are. Many years' experiments and financial investment have gone into the 'science' of marketing and communications management. This is almost a set of faiths in its own right. Different practitioners and corporations may have their own customised practises and language for implementing it, but the core set of beliefs and "commandments" which were created and installed in the first half of the twentieth century by brand builders survive broadly unscathed today. The science is itself a de facto religion, and like all religions, has a strong and enduring will to live on. Religions, like marketing, survive by the 'stickiness' they can create and sustain.

This is about adopting the 'stickiness' of the way we are wired up.

Just when we thought we were moving on from the past, what we find is that religion is less about particular characters and stories, and more of a description for the collective way in which we all appear to be hard-wired into taking easy options by adopting, following, and regurgitating received "wisdom" about the way things are, whether that is in the business of day-to-day living, or the living through of the businesses we find ourselves in.

Religion is a highly adaptable form of virus, a highly effective meme, dedicated to surviving by utilising its hosts as a carrier of its own future, which probably sounds a bit harsh to those who believe in creationism. [1] Marketing behaviour by collectives of brand managers and their supporting and surrounding services continues to display many of the fundamental traits of evolved religions, but because marketing since the 19th century is still 'new', like many technologies, the speed at which it has been able to adopt the lessons of the past and distribute its new message, has been entirely in line with contemporary developments. What used to take centuries can now be done in decades. Let's also not forget that the idea of religion, while dominated through definitions as being the belief in and worship of superhuman controlling powers, also gets to be defined in two further ways – as a particular system of faith and worship, and as a pursuit or interest followed with devotion, which conveniently can also secularise it.

But let's soften the blow for the purposes of experimentation, and once again take the observation out of the front-line of those waging the war for branded market share, profit, and kudos, and look at a parallel example to demonstrate the transferability of this notion without immediate damage to sensitive brand representatives.

The last four years of activity in the financial services sector acts as a fascinating insight into the future awaiting marketers who still think the only way forward is to a never-ending world of more and more passionate and emotionally engaged brands, profit, and intangible fame.

Like with the Halo Effect,[2] we saw, shortly after the unlearned lessons of the dot.com bubble, a further round of behaviour in financial markets where magicians pulled innumerable rabbits from magic hats, and most of the audience looked on in amazement, all seemingly secretly wishing and hoping and, well, faithfully knowing, there would be another one still coming out. It is hard to overstate the power of group thinking in business and finance[3]. Here was a world where people routinely listened out for the latest hot tip or view about market modelling and behaviour, and as long as they heard someone else also pass around the 'fact', they regarded it all as gospel, a new testament. It was cool if you could count yourself as in with the trendy thinkers and market makers. It became the norm to follow convention, even if convention says go with the high risk, go with a complex product whose underlying formula you can't really fathom. There is a divine circle of knowing shining in the sky, not a cloud of unknowing to cast doubt, and thousands of sun and star worshippers flocked to embrace the light, refusing to acknowledge the development of the storm clouds building on the horizon. Distorting lenses were propagated everywhere. If you didn't go with the crowd and buy the shades that let you look cooler under the sun you were out. What was true was what was believed, and what was believed was true[4].

And so it is the same for marketing, but before we return to that, take another observation from the world of economics, where it was deemed that it is better for your career to be conventionally wrong than unconventionally right[5].

In the marketing world, the trend over scores of years or more was to undergo the right of passage conferred by a quality MBA, such that one joined a marketing priesthood at the fast-track level rather than having to undergo the boring roots-up entry process through grubbing around in things like sales and talking to retailers and consumers directly.

No MBA credentials? No membership of the elite. It became like a world with guilds and orders to match the pomposity and arrogance of the Middle Ages, as well as the protectionism, with about as much the same levels of insight into reality, and with the same disproportionate rewards for sacrificing one's judgement, or at least one's opinion, to the greater good, ie.an accelerated career path, title, role, status, and, maybe, immense compensation.

"What difference will you make in the world?" is the question Harvard Business School asks its students. Well, some of its alumni are names like John Thain and Stan O'Neal, Andy Hornby and Hank Paulson, Rick Wagoner, Jeffrey Skilling, and George Bush. OK, so that's just a spoonful from the bowl that has produced 70,000 or more graduates, but their high-profile contributions to the subject of leadership raises a number of questions about elite values, rewards, and business and personal ethics, depending entirely on your perspective and observations points.

In the early stages of their careers it was people like those mentioned above who caused flocks of others to invest in MBAs for themselves, their families and futures, and many are probably hard-working people in their respective industries today. But they are often not open-minded to new solutions that may just re-value their businesses and their roles in a downward direction. Too many of them are driven by what might be described as the logic of quantification, a need to reduce the world to a set of things that can be measured, containing a version of reality in a goldfish bowl, and consigning the hard to measure to a dark world beyond the lights directed at the pretty tropical fishes in the impressive lobby

As it was said of financial markets, the 'mind of the market' is very powerful[6].

When the collective view has been established, challenges to it are resisted. So it is not surprising when challengers to the religion of marketing meet with scorn and derision. After all, to take a number of well-rewarded roles for intelligent people out of the mix is a serious business, even if they can be shifted to other contributory roles. People don't give up the trappings of status easily, and certainly not on moral pleading grounds if they have contracts in jurisdictions where the law is robust, and beliefs are stronger.

At this point it becomes clear then that to keep railing against these kinds of faiths, shored up with sophisticated intellectual defenders and the kind of money that secures effective defence lawyers if matters come to court, it might actually not be the best way forward, unless you are going to live to be as old as Noah to see something through. It must also be acknowledged that most religions appear to be capable of mustering considerable amounts of patience as they wait for their ultimate dominance to prevail over time.

So, in the spirit of religious conformity, and a desire to survive, rather than die under some form of Marketing Inquisition, let's adopt what we rail against in our favour. With today's communications technology and speed of adoption, we should be able to compress centuries of effort into a very compact time-frame and see what benefits we can create quickly.

What a radical idea, like 'Protest – Antism' was. What can we call on to base our faith upon? What can we use to chastise false Gods and their surroundings and trappings? What can be our testament? What can be our commandments?

Well, our kind of 'faith' is based on

Simplicity

That's it.

If that's too difficult, or not sufficiently intellectually inspiring, there's a half-way house entry point that Einstein was keen on, – that is, make everything as simple as possible, but no simpler.

So, in the spirit of effective precedents, here are our ten commandments to guide us to a more effective and rewarding future:

1. Learn what to ask, and how to ask it.
2. Dig deep and learn to look in the right places.
3. Don't waste time.
4. Work especially hard to make things simple.
5. Test all propositions for credibility with yourself.
6. Encourage and respect others' contributions.
7. Challenge mediocrity.
8. Remember how to enjoy things.
9. Share.
10. Don't be frightened of saying 'I don't know, maybe you could

help me understand'.

What might life look like if we take these propositions out into our markets and on to our brands?

Our belief is that it makes the practise of both marketing and communications faster, more enjoyable – and more effective.

Let's take a moment to think about why that might be:

The pursuit of complexity.

A lot of people are employed at not-insignificant cost in marketing and communication services. If you are paid well, it goes without saying that what you do is important. If it is important, then that means it must require the exercise of significant intellect. And in some markets too, our own egos dictate that what we do has significant meaning and value.

If we are employed in marketing coffee or cornflakes, we don't like to think that all there is to it is to tell people about why our coffee or cornflakes are good, and let them make their own decisions. We want to consider all potential avenues and pitfalls in order to determine how best to prove that our product is the best.

Then too, in western 'alpha male' society, it's important that our peer group understands the value of what we do for the greater good.

Significant desk work is required, plus research and deep psychological understanding of the meaning of a cup of coffee in our day, and its potential to change our behaviour – and before we know it, we have a process that commonly lasts 48–64 weeks from the inception of a brief to the appearance of a piece of communication. Along the way, endless group sessions will have been held to uncover and discuss every possible strategic option, before getting into any creative process.

No one thinks to apply the 80/20 rule – let's get the brief 80% right, start work, and refine it as we go along from there. So a discussion about whether, for example, the word 'stimulate' is better than 'invigorate', or is better than 'rejuvenate', could take many weeks. And why is that? Do we really believe any normal consumer going about their daily life will stop to ponder the difference? And will it make any difference?

Charles Handy once opined of a leading UK advertising agency when asked for a point of view on working practises that he observed a lot of very intelligent people making the apparently simple complex, primarily for their own amusement.

Our own point of view is that there is much truth in this. So we would contend that if we could begin to embrace the notion of simplification, it would have an immediate effect on the speed at which we operate and bring recommendations to market.

It's a serious business we work in.

Somewhere along the way we have become confused about the difference between achieving objectives and how we get there. Marketing has become serious and not something to be taken lightly. Humour is for less serious topics.

And we really wonder if that has to be the case?

Happy workers are more productive, more committed, willing to work late when necessary. It seems to us that the application of a bit more 'real world' to day-to-day practices might have the dual benefit of putting things into a better and more useful perspective – and making things a bit more enjoyable.

In a recent working day we saw a meeting report that in the same sentence indicated an embryonic piece of creative work lacked emotional resonance and dictated the inclusion of visual legal mandates, and if that is not an oxymoronic request, what is? We pointed this out to the author of the document, intending to amuse them – they responded by asking us not to "mock". How did we come to a place where humour and fun has so little place in the work environment?

Do as I say........

We have referred earlier in this book to the emergence of 'inclusivity of thinking' as a key factor driving marketing group behaviour. As in any religion worth its salt, it is often not encouraged in the communications environment to ask too many questions or challenge sacred cows.

But in our view, it is never wrong – and often very right – to ask someone to explain why they hold a particular point of view, or why they have issued a particular request. Just because they hold a senior position does not mean they are omniscient or omnipotent. They may be the principal decision-maker, but they are unlikely to be in possession of all relevant facts or information at any given point in time. It is the job of others in the team to ensure that the Team Leader has the right and most relevant data available to make well-informed decisions – and sometimes, this does not always happen, so requests are made and briefs issued which may not make perfect sense to someone in possession of other intelligence.

That's why it's important to ask if something doesn't make sense.

That's why you should never criticise someone for asking, "Why?"

That's why each and every culture must find a way to permit and reward individuals who 'dare' to ask the question, "Why?"

It often uncovers new perspectives which enable more timely or relevant thinking on any given topic.

Not all communication is actually effective, and we should strive to make more of it so.

This is our single biggest objective when we call for simplification.

In our experience, making things complex rarely results in more effective communications – or indeed more relevant brand 'experiences'. And that is what we should all be aiming to achieve.

It is not easy to prove that communications are effective. Given all the activity globally, the scant number of brands rewarded with either an Effie or an IPA Advertising Effectiveness Award bears witness to the difficulty of "proving" effectiveness. But that is what we all seek – and common sense dictates that we accept that much communication activity does not result in different behaviour, or changed attitudes towards a brand. A lot of it is probably not even noticed.

So it seems to make sense to us to apply some common sense. If what you are proposing to say does not make sense to you, why should it to anyone else?

This led us to formulate our principles of simplification, which we reiterate below. They seem to us to make a good foundation for thinking about brands and their communication in a more relevant and compelling way.

In the next chapter, we have applied the principle of 'real world simplification' to a new way to think about brands.

1. Learn what to ask, and how to ask it.

2. Dig deep and learn to look in the right places.

3. Don't waste time.

4. Work especially hard to make things simple.

5. Test all propositions for credibility with yourself.

6. Encourage and respect others' contributions.

7. Challenge mediocrity.

8. Remember how to enjoy things.

9. Share.

10. Don't be frightened of saying 'I don't know, maybe you could help me understand.'

9. A Simpler Way to Work with Brands More Effectively

Here we focus on applying the principles of 'real world simplification' we set out at the end of the last chapter, to thinking about how to deal with brands in the context of people's lives.

We are going to build a model that is easy to understand and work with. It can be carried around in your head, and easily shared with lots of others. It is faithful to the principles we have just set out. Whether you accept the thinking or not, this approach makes it worthwhile for introducing a wider range of people, thinking and effective contributions to brand destinies without the dominance of one particular form of coercive egotism. Even where such behaviour still dominates, this model can illustrate ways for realigning a number of challenged brands successfully with users.

We are building a different way of looking at brands, a way to simplify things, not to make things appear even more esoteric. We acknowledge the difficulty of trying to capture entireties, but reflect the need to use simple demonstrations to offer meaning in what otherwise might appear to be impossibly complex, or even contrarian, situations. This is the kind of approach that helped such insightful scientists as Richard Feynman to communicate the fascination of the quantum world to a wide audience.

Let's reflect this by creating our first territory, or space, for brands to exist in, the first of four such territories, in this brand universe. This territory we call – Life Support Brands.

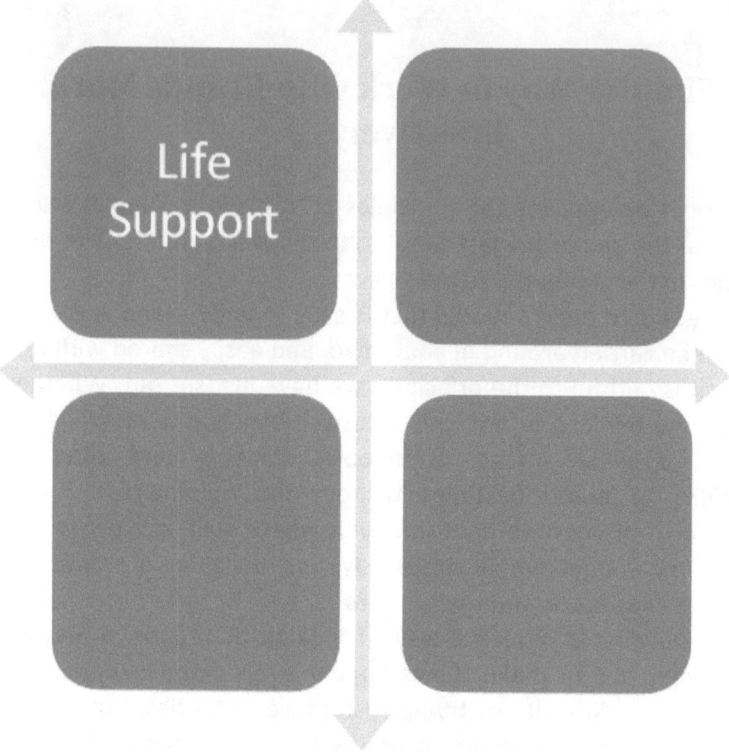

Life Support Brands

Here we are, in our first territory. Let's look around and get acquainted with it. Life Support Brands help us get on with our lives at basic levels. These brands are best at functional performance. They clean us, feed and wake us, protect us, cover us, and generally help us through each day, giving us room and time to get on with all those other things we have elected to do. If our day only has time for the basics, they make life easier, and some manufacturers try to make them more affordable for us. These brands are essentially functional.

But this doesn't mean we don't like these brands, because we do. They help us, day to day. It's just that we value their functional delivery on a pragmatic basis, more than having some externally-created emotional relationship imposed on us.

Maybe one of the best examples of recognition of this insight comes from our often quoted Ronseal, with its "Does what it says on the tin" communication. Brave indeed in a world where many other products are trying to insist that their selection and application will ensure you will be deemed successful, wise, and enamoured by the opposite sex if only you choose them, as opposed to making sure that the garden fence won't just turn into wood chips next week.

These are brands we can buy which are to all intents and purposes 'passive' i.e. we don't need to interact with them at high levels of emotional engagement because they deliver functionality consistently, and that's what we need. It is this functionality that brand communications need to concentrate on, and this which will earn our respect or displeasure. Brands whose functionality wavers are rewarded or punished by their distance from perceived or actual performance benchmarks that are tacitly held in users' heads, borne out of experience or word-of-mouth-fuelled expectation. So the detergent brand that damages clothes is punished by brand switching, until it re-emerges at an acceptable level of functionality, when it may be reconsidered and used, or it slips off the scale again. We are not talking about renewed wedding vows here.

A brand that has lost its lustre can still enjoy being a healthy business if it can earn respect based on acceptable levels of functionality – it doesn't need everlasting fame or celebrity to exist, nor expensive communication support systems to fuel it. Yet it still needs wise management. Getting the most out of these brands requires first-class skills, action and behaviour. There should be no guilt that these brands are not worth as much attention as other brands – they don't need it. Their managers should be rewarded through the incremental brand value they have identified in eliminating wastage or redundancies, managing the brand at realistic levels of engagement and connectivity.

In today's world, Reckitt Benckiser is a company that has understood this well. Its managers are rewarded for delivering excellence within the boundaries outlined above. Cillit Bang may at one level have been just another household cleaning brand, but its functionality was such that it commanded a formidable (price) premium positioning in its market, and delivered high margin and sustained growth, even in mature European markets.

There are implications for how you communicate with users as a life support brand. As we have indicated above, much time and effort has been spent over the last forty years trying to identify relevant emotional benefits for many of these kinds of brands, very often

133

relating to the emotional well-being of an idealised and now increasingly rare nuclear family, and then turning this into communications. So we witnessed the creation of the 'Perfect Mum' as a result of using whatever product was being advertised. Even in the long-running series of Oxo ads that attempted to capture a more realistic portrayal of life as it is actually lived, when they began back in the early 1980s they injured many sacred cows by featuring a reasonable version of the reality of stereotypical family life (i.e. mild arguments), with Linda Bellingham playing the role of a Mum, but she still always came out on top. And not a lot has changed since then.

In our view, such attempts to graft emotional relationships onto products that, if we are honest, users use on a daily basis without giving much thought about them at all, is wasteful in terms of both time and money. People are perfectly happy with these branded goods, without the communication fraternity turning to what is effectively emotional blackmail to try to build loyalty and commitment.

So we can revert to a much simpler model, in many cases freeing up valuable time and money to invest elsewhere − in product development, for instance, or realistic pricing in developing markets. Increasingly, users 'punish' brand owners for poor functionality and/or poor perceived value for money.

We are making some general observations about the implications for communications that fall out from what we are calling 'Keeping It Simple', based on empirical cases. We would point out that a book of at least equal length to this one could be produced on the whole topic of media strategy and execution in relation to this classification, and we welcome the media community's continuing work to manage how to get the best out of the proliferation of media or communication channels, and to increase the understanding of how existing media and emerging channels are used and combined. These are simply observations to keep the debate alive, and to move forward productively.

Communications for life support brands should focus on strong functionality and product delivery. These brands do need 'to work' - users will no longer forgive weak functionality, disguised in a fake emotional promise. So let's celebrate the fact that they do work.

The role of television advertising for all but a few 'power brands' is questionable on an on-going basis. It may be justifiable to announce 'news' or deliver key pieces of information – but the messages should be simple, and to the point. Again, as we have said before, a Ronseal-type message – "Does exactly what it says on the tin" – is a brilliant role model. Other channels and media can be leveraged much more potently than they are currently. Recognising that levels of 'active emotional engagement' with brands in this quadrant are not going to be very high, necessarily, communication should be simple and clear – focusing on relevant information.

When Cillit Bang was launched in Europe it quickly became a cult cleaning product. Its communication focused on the eradication of massive amounts of dirt, something which other brands had been too timid to do. The amount of dirt shown was unprecedented. It quickly attracted the attention of a group of users who had not historically been closely linked with cleaning - men. Women users, in focus groups, reported that they had purchased the product because their husbands had told them to. The company took that recommendation onto the internet – in the form of happy customer endorsement via blogs. Who would have thought it?

What remains dangerous in going down this route is the weight of opposition that comes from established practice. Who wants to be a life support brand? It's not a real brand is it, it doesn't have high rates of emotional bonding?

But there are many widely powerful global brands in existence today which allow us to question the need for every brand to offer an emotional benefit. Google is one that springs to mind. We are not talking about trust – that is a given, every brand has to be trusted to deliver its core competence or benefit. But the increasingly out-dated notion that we should regard every brand as a person, with its own dominant character – and that consumers somehow have to be emotionally engaged with each and every brand they come into contact with, is naïve.

These resistances to change are normal. A few will notice an opportunity, performance will look good, and the adoption curve will steepen.

Let's travel into another part of the universe, into another territory.

This is the territory occupied by what we call Bartering Brands.

Bartering Brands

These are brands that 'talk' to you, have a dialogue with you, and where you have a more dynamic interaction with them. They often require some form of interaction because many of them offer services that help you, say, travel from a to b, or manage your money more effectively, or, through the information and service they provide, enable you to make considered decisions about what directions and choices you might make in your life. Once again, these don't have to occupy stretched emotional dimensions, and in fact where they try, they often fail. Look at the number of attempts financial services organisations have made to show their caring side, only to then withdraw services and support when the rain begins. These brands would do better to give you what you want without the dressing, because they are there to satisfy your needs based on the trade between the information they have, and the information or service you seek. This is the element of the barter.

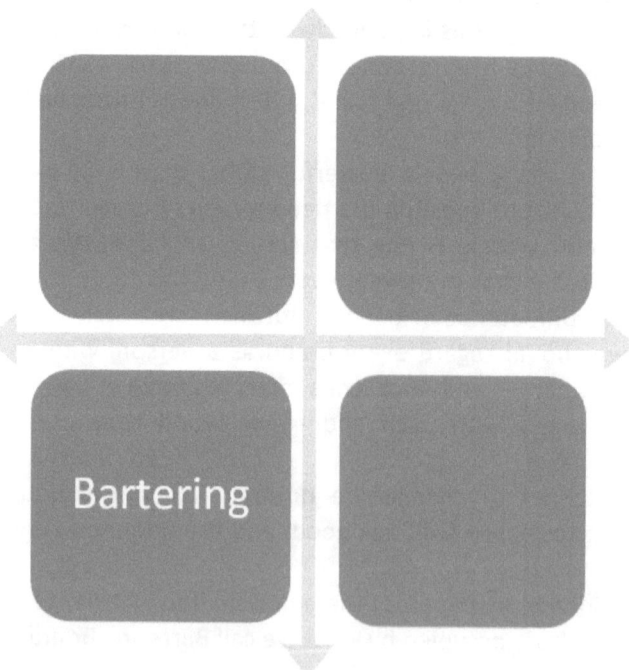

Let's look at this second quadrant in more detail. These bartering brands try to satisfy needs and often have complex functionality, but what separates them from life support brands is that there are higher levels of interaction required with them to get a result. Brands like this usually offer a range of options, providing a degree of tailoring for individual or group needs, and a combination of range and flexibility often gives them a functional edge. Things like cost-comparison sites, airline deal travel search sites, on-line supermarket shopping sites, or, in real places, department stores with help desks, ticket sales outlets, travel agents. Different brands may come to mind offering different levels of service or attention, but the majority of them live in a recognisable part of the universe.

All brands, however much they concentrate on what they believe is a focused type of performance, do not sit precisely in one spot in a territory. They orbit around their space, some in wide orbits, some others in tightly packed ones. This is because of the effect of different observers on them, and users of them, coupled with the effects of perspective, diffraction, and context that all also come into play.

In our emerging model, product categories exist in a dominant territory or quadrant in which most category brands orbit. There are always exceptions, and the temptation for many brand custodians is to define themselves as exceptions, seeking out a place in the wrong territory, or space. Some exceptions work, but most should get comfortable with the space they have come to live in, or more naturally belong in, and get the most out of those conditions, finding a suitable orbit that potential users, or loyalists can clearly spot.

How brands are seen and regarded really does depend on both the position of the observer who doesn't have to be stationary, and the lenses through which they see a brand. A brand's orbit may take it close to another territory or deeper within its own territory, depending on the user or observer, but its dominant orbit will never simultaneously occupy two or more quadrants.

The point here is to acknowledge that the observations of brand managers and brand users are often going to be different, so views on how and where brands are positioned or should be seen need constant and careful measurement and correction. If there are gross distortions, diffractions, or disagreements about territories and the general shape and pattern of orbits, then those reveal areas where profitable work can probably be done.

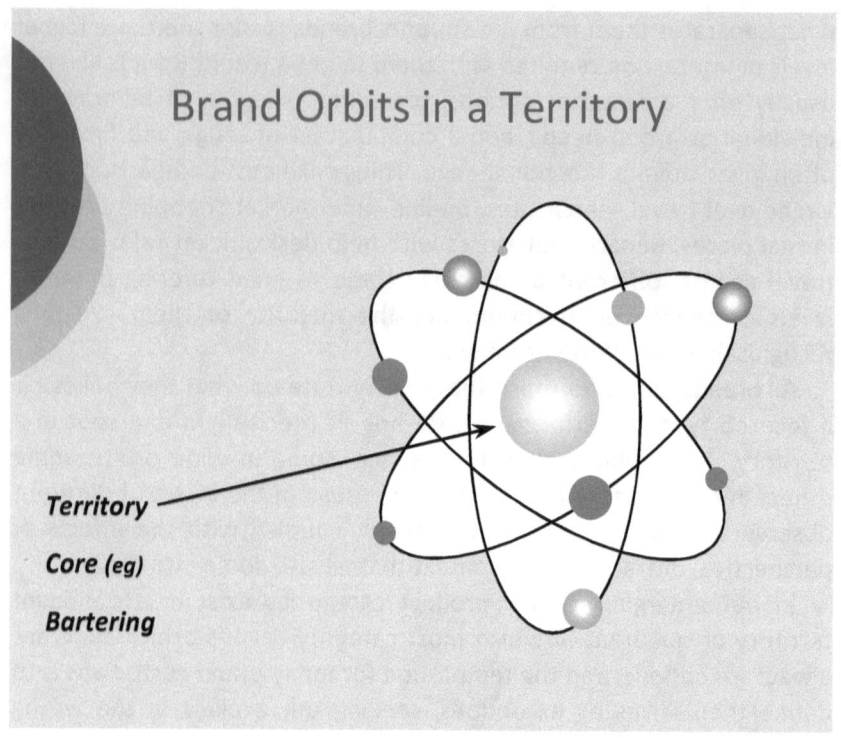

Brand Orbits in a Territory

Territory

Core (eg)

Bartering

This is especially true of bartering brands that are used to construct a product, service, or experience which you co-create. To reprise, bartering brands are the ones where you are not simply purchasing a product that is otherwise sitting passively on a shelf or on a floor. The territory these brands occupy can be very large, and their orbits complex.

For example, a user might book into a hotel on a Wednesday for a business meeting on a Thursday and Friday. This guest wants a seamless check-in, no fuss, the meeting room sorted, the presentation facilities hooked up and working. After a successful meeting, the same guest may decide to stay on for the weekend. This user then switches from productivity mode to pamper-me mode, and expects the service delivery to be able to recognise and meet this need. Brands like this clearly get more points when they can easily identify the shift in need and satisfy it at a price and level judged by the user to be worth the return in service.

The person sitting next to you on the airplane may have paid more than you for a seat, but may still be happier than you in the context of the way the seat was bought i.e. it was cheaper than the price offered by a competitor, which they thought constituted a bargain at the time of purchase. You paid one euro plus taxes, but you were free to travel any time. The person who flew in the Gulfstream V will also justify the expense by bundling up the totality of costs/time saved i.e. convenience of departure and arrival times, plus accessibility to smaller or closer airports to where business is being done, plus hours saved which has a big impact on their hourly charge-out rate, and so on. Or they may not bother with the calculation because they have so much money it's not worth fussing over. There used to be a game called "How much money would have to be lying on the sidewalk for it to be worthwhile for Bill Gates to stop and pick it up?"

A brand's value here is totally relative to your specific needs today. One person's Emirates is another's Ryanair, and so on.

These bartering brands meet needs, and some have degrees of emotional connection, but this is still less important than the functionality they deliver. Like banks, credit card companies have tried for years to build emotional relationships with you, and then just when they start to get close they do something like declare service charge hikes and substantially increased profits while telling you your card usage will now be restricted to protect you from fraud, all the while forgetting it's you who granted them the privilege of service in the first place. Airlines can have drinks in plastic sachets or caviar and gold-plated seat belt buckles, but they are still only as useful as the routes they service. It may be good to know there are some of the world's finest wines being ruined at 35,000 feet, but if you're not going to Asia any time soon, so what?

Life support brands thought they had a chance to claim service credentials when the Internet rolled up. It was fashionable to think and believe that a life-support brand could be the portal to many of your other wants and needs. As we noted, you'd always want to order your groceries and holidays through your essential floor-cleaning brand, wouldn't you? Wouldn't you?

Brands as gateways have soaked up millions of dollars and strategic rationales as they have pushed and shoved to be your connection to the world's sweet spots. But a brand can't be anything its manager wants it to be. That's just a brand manager tail trying to wag an expectant brand user dog. But loads of people have seriously tried to give their brands more status, or a bigger presence, or a bigger role, in this kind of way.

Bartering brands do open things up for you, but they are not the final destination. If a flight was the best part of your holiday, unless you are on an aviation enthusiasts' holiday, it doesn't say much about the holiday. As with life support brands, bartering brands can afford to spend more time improving the quality of their functional delivery, and less time on creating wish-fulfilment images that empirically many users recognise for what they are – fictions, and not compelling ones at that.

So some of the views that would apply to communications for life support brands also apply to bartering brands.

Users are more interested in factual information and dependable delivery than having an emotional relationship with bartering brands.

As observed earlier, many of the High Street banks have spent millions of pounds over the last 30 years trying to persuade us that they are our best friends and have our best interests at heart – but realistically, nothing has really changed, and very few of us believe that banks have anything other than their own interests at heart.

If we are honest with ourselves, pretty much the same is true of how we think we relate to insurance companies, car hire companies, and some supermarket chains. So communication that seeks to try to do more than communicate the functional at this level, brilliantly, may well not represent best value.

The critical point of delivery here is the product experience itself. If this does not deliver, then no amount of communication, no matter how persuasive, will retain customer loyalty for long. Better to invest in improved product delivery in these cases. Communication should generally be transparent and honest, a challenge for some players. Just try to recall one service ad like this from your perusal of the paper or your on-line media this morning, that is, where you didn't elect to screen out advertising messages altogether.

One area where there is an opportunity to keep a step ahead is to allow customers to make their own recommendations within the service brand's web-site and other on-line services. Personal recommendation is a key driver of usage of many of these kinds of brands. 47% of holidays booked with one leading UK travel agent were booked as a result of personal recommendation, and brands which have the courage to ask their customers to comment within their official web-site rather than via a blog may well be in a position to prosper to the detriment of their less courageous competitors.

We may now continue on our space-rocket journey, and enter a third territory. This third territory, or quadrant, we call Complementarity Brands.

Complementarity Brands

We are now in a space where function and a certain set of emotions embrace each other more clearly. There are many brands with which people continue to have emotional relationships, and here is one of the densest galaxies in the universe. It is also one where thousands of brand owners and managers have invested energy in creating values for what they cherish or hope are their brand stars. Let's go inside one of these star factories.

After the two day off-site session, covering the wall in post-it notes and getting-to-know-you exercises, the essence of the brand is finally captured: 'Earth – the place to Live.' In some enterprises there would then be another session to discuss whether a line like that really would deliver if the definite article had to be italicised, and anyway, how will it translate into French? Eventually they decide on 'Earth – where it's at, and the French opt for 'France is the best place on Earth'. Versions of this are being played out every day.

Then we re-visit brand personalities. Like our old world of Kodak, they do not necessarily embrace a large part of the real world. Brands are always 'friendly, open, trustworthy, caring, responsible, energetic, and of course, fun', like the workshops. This is gross redundancy. We reiterate, who is ever going to keep defining their brand in terms of the opposite of these, 'unfriendly, close-minded, dishonest, uncaring, irresponsible, lethargic, and dull'?

The codes of established practice here are tarnished and tired. Like make-you-a-celebrity shows, the point of entry must include versions of this – "I had a terrible childhood, this is the greatest challenge of my life, this is my one chance to live my dream, I don't know what I'll do if I don't get this". In the old days it was girls in bikinis wearing a sash and declaring to the presenter that "I love children, I am so happy, I want peace for the world" in a phonetically-learned and practised English.

Brands that are edgy, or moody, are unlikely to be life support brands. Some bartering brands can go there, but where these approaches are more likely to flourish is in this quadrant – our Complementarity Brands.

Complementarity brands cross the line between needs and wants. One person might describe a moisturiser as something they need, another as something they want. A $100 moisturiser will segregate the need/want users further, as they see it from different places. A brand with a complementarity orbit may tangentially touch the life support territory, but the $100 brand is going to be a want brand for all but a few. The wealthy can justify the brand purchase as an essential need, a life support need, but that is minority observance. The current view of most brand-connected employees is still today that a brand "says something about you", or that you and the ideal brand co-exist in a mutually supportive world of admiration.

This is the area where many 'want' brands come to define their existence. Functionality may be a part of their performance, but they also embrace values like love, self-esteem, aspiration, achievement or status, more than life support brands and honestly appraised bartering brands. This remains confusing for some by the fact that so many brands today still lay claims to qualities they don't or can't really possess in the opening eyes of users.

While complementarity brands themselves might also offer services, these work principally to reinforce your worthiness for inviting them 'to dignify their existence with your presence'. Complementarity brands make you feel good about yourself and subsequently maybe others, and they spend a lot of time working on ways in which their value and values match yours. Complementarity brands are big on intangible value. They love words like cachet and charisma, magic and mystique, hand-crafted and designed. Complementarity brands need to stay on top of their game in terms of their total product offer, as people who buy these brands will happily switch to other brands if they perceive a more interesting or innovative product promise linked to an emotional message.

This quadrant is closer to the accepted wisdom in communication agencies about brand development and communication than any of the others, by dint of the fact that users generally do want to have an emotional connection with these brands, but increasingly this is on their own terms, not the brands' terms.

Brands here often try to say a lot about who you are, and many fashion and beauty brands are located here. Not so long ago, you might have believed Rimmel as an entry level, cheerful cosmetic brand for teenagers. It might have been a life support brand. Today after a make-over and effective sponsorship from Kate Moss, it has been for millions of teenage girls a complementarity brand.

As indeed was Dove, from Unilever. This was the brand that for a time effectively turned a mass-market moisturiser into a beauty icon for millions of women, by turning on its head conventional wisdom about the nature of beauty. Its 'Real Beauty' campaign eschewed the stereotypical imagery of beautiful women, and used real women, sometimes of large proportions, to demonstrate its philosophy that beauty comes from within. It was a brave move, and a brave client who bought into such an unconventional approach.

So this quadrant is not restricted to prestige brands, although many of them do sit here. It has just as much relevance to brands that play a less sophisticated role in our everyday lives, yet still make contributions to our dreams and aspirations. For those tempted to propose that their household cleaning product has suddenly found a role as a complementarity brand, think again. The only people who think like that are brand managers, and many don't apply the same criteria to themselves outside the office anyway. There is a need for a reality check. There is a difference between passion and commitment about the brands we work on, and appropriate levels of realism, without diluting energy, enthusiasm, or career-building activity.

Complementarity brands must still be able to perform, but they can perform with functionality that can be based on product ingredients and/or emotional delivery.

It also pays, if you are the owner of a wide portfolio of brands, to give attention to making sure that the right hand knows what the left hand is doing. Not so long ago Unilever was accused[11] in a user-generated viral ad, of exploiting young women via another of its portfolio of brands (Axe/Lynx). It may well be that this was not intentional, or that users had effectively misunderstood the intended style of the advertising, i.e. tongue in cheek, but nonetheless this shows that it is dangerous to under-estimate the ability and willingness of today's users to form and publish or broadcast their own judgements on brands and brand owners, within portfolios of products. Brands are no longer ring-fenced from each other and their parent companies, and neither are their product ranges.

Jack Welch once dramatically summed up the challenge to deliver excellence at General Electric (GE) when he said, "Why should I buy a jet engine from General Electric in the afternoon when my GE toaster didn't work at breakfast?"

In another world, one of the views of Royal Dutch Philips was, why buy stuff from others if we can make it ourselves and sell it? So they ended up with 20,000 products, from rice cookers to toilet seats to market leading medical scanners. But once you can't be the best at everything you turn your hand to, you need to be careful.

Complementarity is clearly not just for the ladies. The last fifteen years has seen the burgeoning of many male complementarity markets, from male grooming to dedicated vanity magazine products, fitness and health enhancement systems, and an ever wider range of bespoke products.

This is a useful place to be, especially if you are trying to justify a premium positioning, but it takes work to become and remain successful here. In our view, many brands today continue to try to compete here when there really is no need or point. Today's consumers ruthlessly punish 'pretenders' in this quadrant – by choosing not to believe, engage and ultimately buy into them. Better to take a long honest look at what your brand really is and what it offers people in the context of their lives, and position it appropriately, than chase a fundamentally inappropriate emotional point of differentiation.

Now we travel through space again into our remaining territory. Our final quadrant and the brands that "live" in it we call Infomotion Brands.

You've got your life support. You've got your doors to the world opening with bartering brands. You've got plenty of complementarity, so what's left?

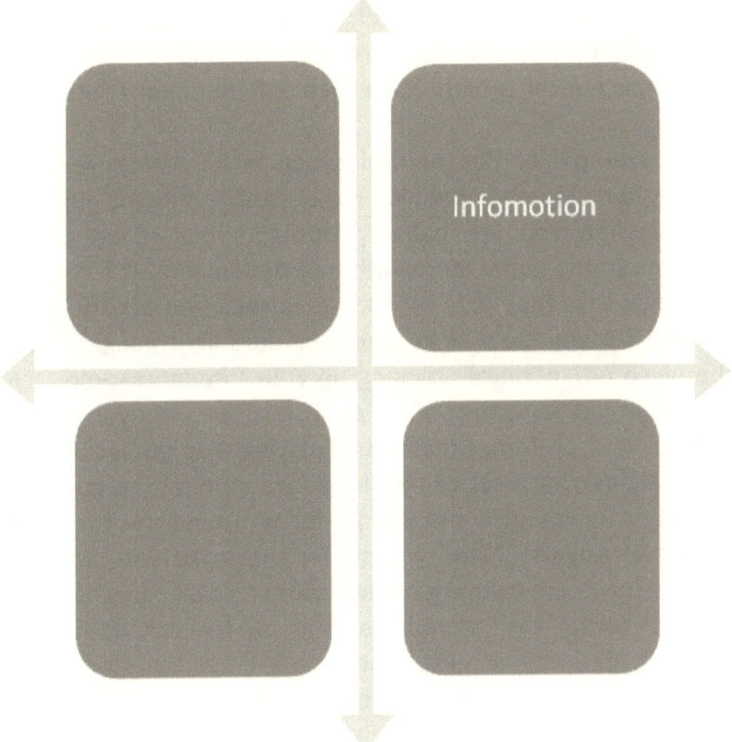

Infomotion Brands

These brands can be like some of those that come to life inside magazines like *T3* and *Hot Stuff*, full of technical wizardry and specialised knowledge. They include both established and innovative technologies, concepts, and detailed technical specifications that mean something special to the deeply involved, informed, or aspirant versions of these. Products like professional digital cameras, the latest mobile handsets, computers, watches, cars, bikes, and anything that celebrates design and engineering ingenuity, are here.

You have a relationship with them that has a degree of emotional attachment, but it is also driven powerfully by the 'informational component of value' they carry, and which you relate to. In this world, what you know and how you are connected have profound implications for your social interrelations and standing, or respect. One orbit might embrace 'geek' factors, and another might tangentially touch complementarity. This is not a male only zone, even if it feels like it on the surface. Some women may have been slightly behind the early manifestations of the tangled Web, but these days they have equally powerful infomotion sites and brands, and a number of expensive cosmeceutical brands have high infomotional content as well.

Here's an example of this part of space in its earlier years of existence. Say you were once the kid who bought an electric guitar. A string breaks when you are halfway through your speed thrash exercise. You go to the guitar store with trepidation and ask for a new E-string. The guy says they only sell strings in sets. You ask for a set. The guy says, "Do you want light gauge or ultra-light gauge?" You, feeling the blush of ignorance creeping up your fifteen year-old face, opt for ultra-light gauge, with confidence. You subsequently learn this is not right for your preferred method of playing. You go back to the store and boldly ask for a set of heavier gauge strings. The guy then says, "Wound or unwound?" and you go for unwound. He then says "Ernie Ball or D' Addario?" and you go for the make you last read about in an old magazine from your elder brother's collection. You fork out $30 and leave the store again in a fug of adolescent embarrassment, determined next time to pre-empt the store guy's omniscience. You get over it by showing off your knowledge to someone who just bought their first guitar and knows nothing, like you did two weeks ago. Today you already have all the data, detail and help you need, not only from your friends, but also from sites that patiently tell you all this information and more, leaving you unembarrassed and able to buy what you want on-line. Welcome to the world of infomotion.

In these worlds, who and what you know are key identifiers of belonging or lack of cool, whatever your gender. Thousands of dollars of premium are commanded by brands that are minutely better than others to distant observers, but infinitely significant to microscopic observers and users. You think the difference in 0-100 kilometre speeds in cars is irrelevant when it's between 4.3 seconds and 3.8 seconds? Getting to the latter figure in the same brand of car, but with the top-end version, is going to cost you an extra $80,000. That's a lot of difference in places where you would be lucky to ever get out of 1st gear.

These brands are not complementarity brands, because they stand up in their own right as objects of desire, whoever their owners are. They don't just complement you. They have an independent existence. A Patek Philippe watch can be had for $10,000, but a grand complication can get you into the hundreds of thousands of dollars bracket, and sometimes even more. You don't wear it just because it flatters you. You have a relationship with its mechanical ingenuity, which can be traded with others as a valuable sign of discrimination and taste. Even the advertising says you only temporarily own the brand, because you will pass it on to your future generations. This is complementarity on one level, but it goes beyond that.

This is not about hierarchies and value around the quadrants. No quadrant is better than another. They are simply places to be, but important ones. The point is that in identifying where you place your brand, your creation, and how you design or map its orbit, you get better returns on your investment if you identify its relationship to users better, and can manage subsequent relationships more efficiently.

Many women have uncanny skills in knowing how much any item of clothing or accessories cost in any season, what is genuine and what is copied, what this year's must have nuances are in a particular designer's handbag, and whose shoes are in or out. This is tacit infomotional knowledge and is used continuously to assess others and one's position in relation to others. A specific bag may then be selected for life support or complementarity reasons, but there are an increasing number of sites that are available to inform or supplement this knowledge in both the bartering and infomotion quadrants.

Infomotion brands can be fleeting, as their components are often rapidly commoditised. They can also become standards of excellence in their own reference frameworks, like Alessi juicers, or Ferrari cars, or can become admired icons over long time frames. Respect for them is not simply aesthetic, it is in the fact that they appear to contain special knowledge that is bigger than the artefact itself. Complementarity brands are devoted to you on your terms. Infomotion brands are always trying to be ahead of you, inviting you to keep up. People enjoy these brands, and the categories they belong to, because they are always pursuing innovation, even if their theme is retrospective.

Let's not forget that men and women still view and approach and use information differently, and this will have an impact on how they see orbits and brands.

Most men will happily plough through pages of technical information on a camera, or a car, but women are much less likely to do so – for them the fact that they are able to recognise this season's "must-have" brand may be enough. This is a much more intuitive skill, though we have noted more and more women now use and enjoy dedicated infomotion categories and services.

Engagement levels with these brands are high, and people will actively seek out information on them, which makes the task of connection much easier. People are actively looking for sign-posts from many of these brands.

Infomotion brands maintain high levels of detail, and fortunately it is the informational component that generates the bonding. It is not a universal unconditional loving relationship for all. The driving reward is in the dynamic interaction of knowing the detail, past, present, and forthcoming.

The point here is that it is the way into the brand that sparks the user's relationship with it. A new high-end Nikon camera will rarely come into the market saying "Check out your holiday snaps with this." It is more likely to declare its ability to capture images better with a high degree of resolution, which you want, and want to know about. The complementarity elements of such brands are consequent to this, not drivers of it

A complementarity brand saying "I'm complex but don't you worry 'cos I'll always be your mate" will often be regarded with disdain by infomotion brand seekers. They don't want the technical stuff taken out.

On the female side, it's a bit like the Pilates 'brand'. For some it's about complementarity, or even life support, but its original entry point was infomotion, it was about detail, about special understanding, about differences from other practices, which were shared among close friends by early users and adopters.

As our Irish friends wisely observe when asked for directions, "To be sure if I was wanting to be going there I wouldn't be starting from here."

Positioning brands and categories in these territories can have profoundly different effects on brand manager behaviour and brand user behaviour.

Where we sensibly choose to understand and accept what our users' relationships with brands really are and should or could be, new value can be recognised and released.

Now it is time to look at the four quadrants together.

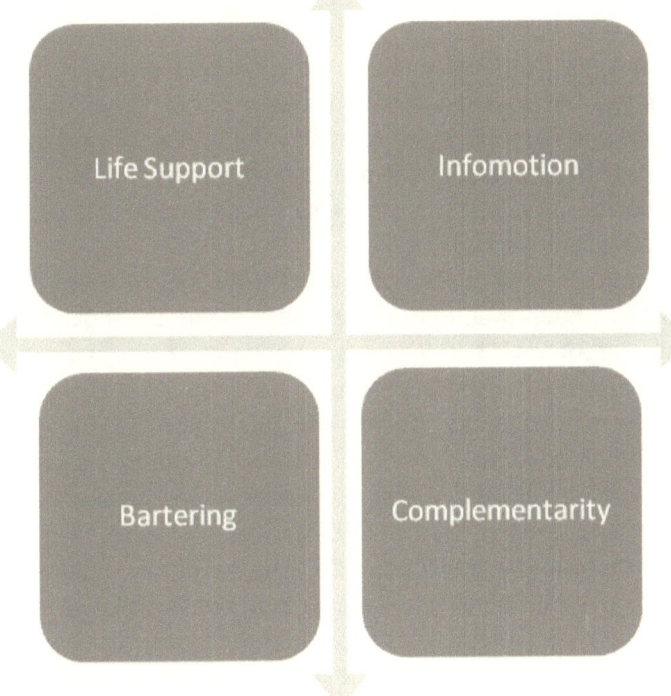

It is critical to ascertain which quadrant a category principally fits in, and then the brands within the category, and what their orbits look like. This will go a long way towards determining what kind of relationships brands need to have to sustain a profitable business, or a worthwhile level of connection with users. Discussion about the category or brand's nature will also enable you to see whether a shift into another quadrant will ultimately be a better prospect for the business, either because it will release more value, or because it has been in the wrong space, and paying the price of miss-occupation.

In our view, for brands to enjoy a better relationship with users, the correct context is king. For years, too many brands have been trying to win a place as complementarity brands in the minds of users when they would have been a lot better off becoming bartering or life support brands. Others have tried to become bartering brands when life support would have been better, and so it goes on.

The quadrants display arrows of expansion, and that is because we want to bring new dimensions into the basic model.

Extra Dimensions

We are going to add two other dimensions to the universe in which the quadrants sit, without creating unwieldy complexity. First we are going to put a need/want dimension over a horizontal axis. This has the effect of gravity. It pulls and stretches the orbits of brands in their quadrants or territories, and explains how someone's 'must have' brand can be perceived as someone else's need brand, and vice versa, as perspectives are tracked.

In this 'universe', the place not to be is at the centre. This is not the black hole we have mentioned, the sweet point of singularity that limits user response, it is simply a place where observers have great difficulty grasping what you are trying to be. As you travel and radiate outwards from the centre, brands can have more of the defining qualities of their quadrants, which gives them differently shaped orbits according to observers' and users' own positions and perspectives.

Unlike many grids of this nature, we re-emphasise, there is no preferred 'best quadrant to be in'. You can be in any quadrant, and have great value. But when you have worked out the best space to be in, concentrate on delivering its representation best. Over zealously delivering values and codes from the wrong quadrant or orbit for you will be costly and confusing. The observers of this kind of action will either spot the flaws or be unsure of the offer, because there will have been a greater level of distortion, or diffraction, than normal.

It has been said that we can only truly count ourselves as fully human when we have learned how to lie, and that this is a fundamental human trait. It is also said that we are very poor at unravelling deception in others, and seeing it for what it is. This insight has enabled people to fool us into buying things, goods and ideas, for millennia. That being said, our final addition to this universe is made up of one further dimension – transparency.

There has never been a better or more necessary time to increase transparency in brands.

We see contrived authenticity all the time. A recent version in time included PR professionals masquerading as private bloggers on the internet, or 'home-made' commercials put out by corporations with deliberately amateur content and styles in an attempt to be authentic. So our final element in binding things together is the quality of transparency. Despite our earlier claim that all good brands must contain trust implicitly, it is only through transparency that trust can be earned, so the days when a brand was automatically supposed to signal trust have been superseded through professional dissembling.

The Internet, in many markets, means that it has never been easier for consumers to check out the honesty of what they are being told by manufacturers, and to pass their experiences on to other like-minded souls, so any desire to obfuscate or be less than open about companies, products or services is generally common knowledge very quickly, and a key driver of public opinion and action.

But remember again in this model, there are no prizes for being in a 'winning' quadrant. All quadrants deliver value, and all quadrants can be motivating to those who choose to work in them, and choose from them. Creative people in grand communication agencies who dismiss things as being boring or not 'proper' brands can simply stay away from those they don't find motivating to work on.

Increasingly, consumers reward brands which address them in their own terms – let's recall Cillit Bang at this point, and the fact that by dint of actually delivering superior cleaning performance, it became the object of a cult blog.

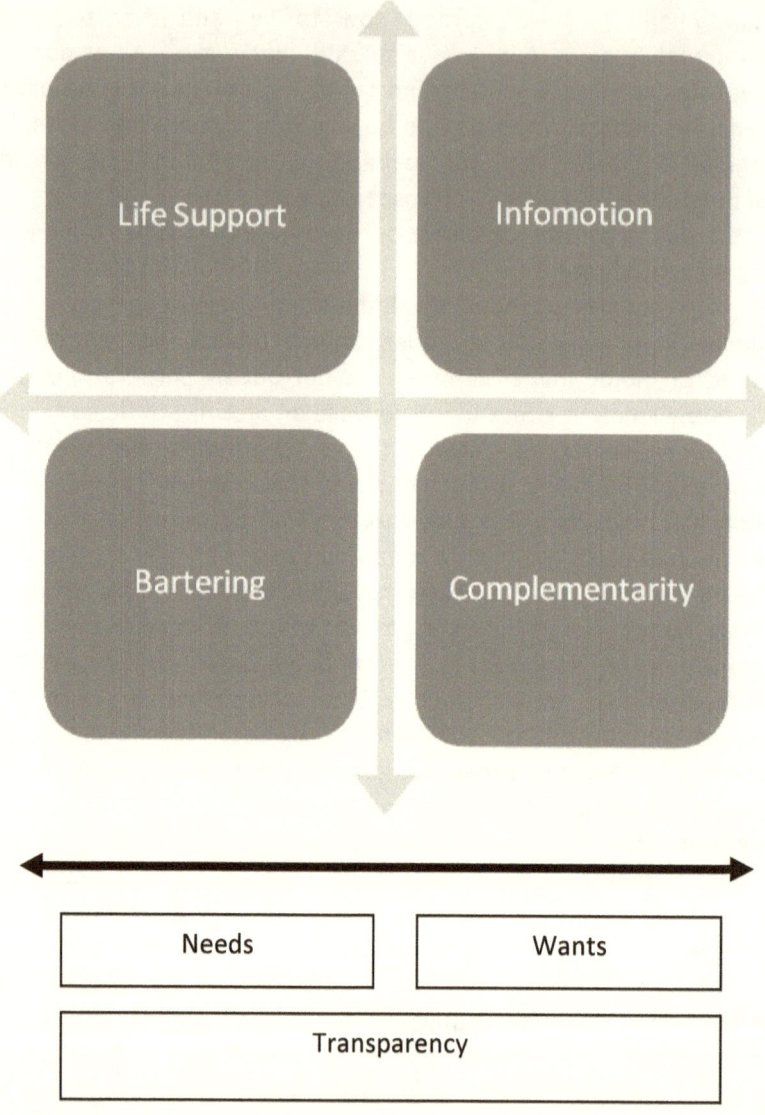

A major additional benefit in this approach lies in the ability to apply and transfer the model to groups beyond the core brand-owning or management entities. Service providers, customers, and users themselves, after a very simple introduction process, can place categories and brands in the model's spaces. Its application is broad and simple. Shifts in placements and orbits can reveal much about brand user/fit and diffraction problems.

Practical working with the model

Because we live in a world where clever people continue to work in marketing and communications businesses, there has been a tendency to create ever more complex formulae and processes to 'get to the bottom' of complex brands. Producing these can be engaging and involving. Getting clients and colleagues to devote the time to understanding them, changing their own adapted processes at length, and adopting new ones for the long term, is a different kind of challenge altogether.

Indeed, in our experience, many worthwhile tools or models fail to succeed because their application to everyday marketing and communication issues is presented as something that you need university level scientific know-how to understand. And in the real world, no one really has much time to do this.

We want our approach to be simple, understandable and easily applicable to problems and challenges. It is, because it is based on how people think, talk about and use brands in the real world.

We are offering tools that can be easily grasped and used, beneficially, almost at once. The tendency is to dismiss such approaches as being too simplistic, missing some kind of magic, or failing to recognise that brands are more sophisticated than all this these days. That's the hard part. We need to improve productivity by getting away from time-wasting analyses of brands' grand roles, and using the time and energy to construct marketing strategies that actually give more back to the relevant relationships brands should have with users. Believe it or not, women today are generally not looking to household cleaning products to assuage their guilt about family cleanliness. Brands that understand this are working very well.

Far too many people have invested time and good money on education courses that make them feel there must be a lot more to it than this. Insightful people need to bring conviction and energy into leading marketing and communication practitioners along a fresh course. This means advocating the need for more simplicity, and the condemnation of redundant complexity and clutter. Data paralysis is leading people to stall action for far too long. This is not an excuse for those with forceful personalities to cut to the chase and say "We'll just get back to doing it my way". Experienced players need to help others use information to shape efficiency, economically, and to drive relevant action.

Our approach means we can get people focused on what brands should be doing, in a real way, quickly. We are not trying to get things right in theory. There is no absolute truth to be found. We must first move, and keep moving, in relative ways. For instance, some research models will advise that it is not recommended to extend brands in certain directions, given their starting point. So the theory goes it is much harder to create a premium product personal product range if your start position is a quasi-commodity, like a bar soap, but easier to introduce quality soaps if your start position is a top-end facial care product or premium skin-care range. Usually the credentials carry you downwards more easily than upwards. You would expect this in oral care too. So who would have thought a toothbrush based brand like Oral-B would be able to get into toothpaste and general oral care from their start-point? Well, Oral-B's owners, Procter & Gamble, seem to think they can. They clearly have some interesting perspectives.

Given that we have said brands are contextualised in people's lives, not the other way round, we would expect very few users to produce models, or orbits, with absolutely equal features. They will look like signatures, or fingerprints, uniquely from that person's perspective, but collective perspectives build up into meaningful and revealing patterns and pictures.

As we have also indicated, brands will not have a point of singularity or a pedestal on which they majestically stand. Their orbits will describe a range and collection of perspectives produced by groups being asked to map the brands on the model. In cases where the predominant shape of the orbits is significantly different from where other mapping groups have placed them, brand managers have the interesting finding of either a lack of fit between their perspective and that of their users, or a view that demonstrates the distortion effects between the management's perspective and the users', or other interested group's perspectives, like suppliers, or retailers.

This exercise in 'comparitivity', or mapping, enables brand owners and managers to decide whether and how to either try to shift their brand orbit, or to try and effect shifts on the perceived orbits of other groups.

In this latter case, orbital shifts might require, in extreme cases, the moving of the brand to another principal category, or role quadrant, altogether. This may be what has been needed for some time. Or it may require the shifting of an orbit closer to another quadrant, or further towards the area where value is maximised. Differences in shifts can lead to understanding whether it is something within the brand, product, or service itself, at the functional level, that is addressable, or whether it is something else, like the brand's communication and 'connectivity' actions with user groups. Either way, this form of modelling rewards those who achieve highly proximate orbits among all observing groups, and helps those where the fit is very different, or diverging, to capture the fact of the matter and elect to do something about it.

Furthermore, since this model can be used at any time, it is worth keeping it in mind as a kind of tracking device, to enable brand management to see whether they are maintaining 'fit' over time, or whether they are beginning to see slippage, at which point it may still be timely and cost efficient to try and help readjust orbits, or the perception of orbits. In this regard the model has additional dynamic features.

In this chapter we have tried to address the critical question, "Do you really believe you have the same relationship with your brand of breakfast cereal as you do with your Porsche?" Many people have worked to try and build emotional bonds of equivalence for their brands, yet intuitively we know this isn't how we really feel about all brands. Our model and approach tries to come to terms with this reality.

Products whose functionality is clear should get on with communicating their functional advantages, or nothing.

Today we live in a changed and still changing world, and in many markets we don't want or need dependent relationships with brands.

Where we sensibly choose to understand and accept what our users' relationships with brands really are and should or could be, new value can be recognised and released.

There has never been a better time to increase transparency in brands.

10. Predictable Barriers to Keeping It Simple

How can we service brand owners and users better? To strip all this down to simple practical levels we need to review briefly some of the things that can get in the way of clarity To begin, let's look at things that were principally fuelled by fortunate years of excess and indulgence, things that created great diversions and distractions, and that need to be managed differently now.

In the distant past, like the late 80s and early 90s, many communication groups were trying to adjust their portfolios to have a large number of multinational accounts, leaving others to build respectable boutique local creative hot shops that could be purchased to add a touch of creative magic dust when the lustre on the monster-sized business was fading slightly. Phrases like 'improved operating margins' were featuring more regularly, and international management groups began to spring up. At least two major conflict areas surfaced, which raged for years

The first one was about control. Who got to control the brands – the international managers or the local managers locally, and in agencies, the local creative directors or the global ones? It may sound obvious but it wasn't easy to work out on the ground. You often got a scenario where international managers were strategy co-ordinators mirroring emerging client structures, with responsibility for a brand but no direct authority to influence staffing or expenditure or bonuses, that resting with regional or local managements. Some executive single client company global creative directors were paid to manage work on an account but had no influence on creative appointments or resource locally. These issues and debates haven't entirely faded.

The second was about power. In many markets anyone who was given an international role was seen as a failure, someone who couldn't cut it in the local creative market. Clients expected their international service people to make organisations deliver to their own new structures and agendas, with often disappointing results. Communication groups that eagerly went round the world following client growth sometimes then found themselves sitting on investments with no returns as clients subsequently shrank operations or revised their reporting structures again. Other clients suffered as, beyond HQ service staff, local service groups were staffed with people the local managers didn't really want, or were saddled with international creative directors who had racks of awards, some rather old, but no real clout within the communication company hierarchy anymore. They were Lifetime Achievement Award Winners. It took years, and several kinds of operating models, before profitable balances were reached in many groups. The search for more productive operating systems continues, with little variation from the rounds of circumstances described above, or to-ing and fro-ing from central to diversified controls and back again.

In WPP, one of the world's largest marketing services groups, Sir Martin Sorrell once said he was installing a growing army of client leaders to manage every aspect of key multinational accounts, and was also nominating country managers. The UK trade journal Campaign noted that "both roles are controversial because operating companies naturally resist the idea of someone who does not report to them having an over-arching responsibility for their clients' business." This was tried in the Disney Corporation, where it once had 'synergy managers' whose role was to get the best out of discrete operating divisions for the good of the whole. Martin Sorrell summed it up, "The thing that bedevils us and our clients is the unwillingness of people to work together". This has been known for decades, centuries even. Still, in many modern client organisations, significant changes are implemented and carried through successfully.[1]

Meanwhile, many brands' destinies were also being shaped by these seismic shifts in operating methodologies. Some companies went for a roster of international brands and shed many local brands, regarding them as now sitting outside a master brand or power brand operating model. Others had international brands with significant local variants. Communication groups attempted to service the spectrum, with various degrees of success. Many advertising agencies that had prided themselves on having their own philosophy were being told that if they didn't hitch their wagon to the client's stated mission and practices there wouldn't be a continuing relationship.

As these changes occurred, another way of looking at the challenges for growth and respect was to get deeper into asking what a creative organisation's intellectual property really should be, and who should be responsible for creating and managing that. A graph that illustrates how advantage may be derived from the proper management of ideas, that we might call Intellectual Property Value, might look like this.

"IP Value Generation Curve"

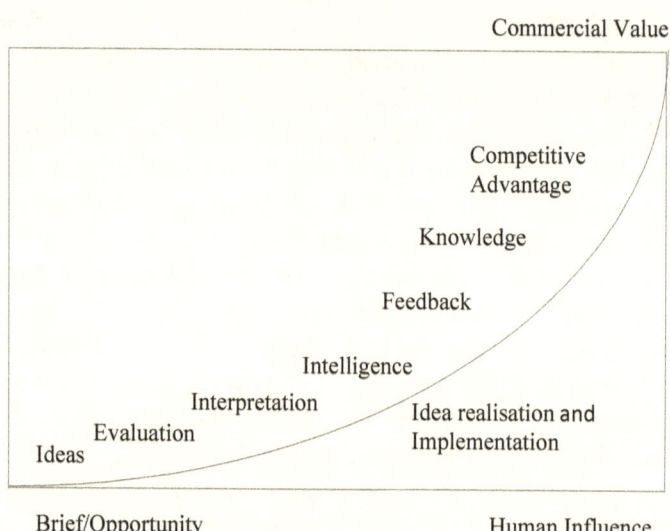

Let's remind ourselves that for most people in marketing and communications environments, an idea is something you see. Whatever most people claim on their home pages, most idea generators remain format or media channel driven. Also, in many cases, ideas are still only supposed to be able to come from creative departments or people with that descriptor in their title. This is in itself a very interesting perspective. A 'Brand Idea' is still one of the hardest things to define in the marketing and communications business. Showing it can be even harder.

A 'Brand Idea' itself seems to be an elusive creature to net, observe, and classify. If it cannot help in building meaningful links with users, it is only an intellectual distillation. It becomes like Winston Churchill's comment about Russia – "a puzzle wrapped up in a problem wrapped up in an enigma", that few can fathom. Some generators of Brand Ideas believed they helped those charged with managing brands to keep focus. Unfortunately, these pithy summaries were still often open to diverse interpretation, allowing widely different actions to take place. Other managers would then say, "That's not what I/we/it mean(s)". No-one was getting help, at great expense.

In Palo Alto, California, decades ago, the Xerox Corporation ran a famed development centre with poets and musicians, mathematicians and logicians, and variations in between, all dreaming up new ideas. Remember Xerox then was a major government supplier, so investment research and development money was plentiful. Some new ideas were exploited by the parent company, and others were picked up by outside players, most notably Apple Computers, who made famous the Mouse – the other one. The point is they had a broad source for ideas. Procter & Gamble recognised this, and realised they were not necessarily getting as many ideas as they might from within their closed operating system. Since 2000 P&G has opened its development programme to the whole world of external developers and experts, with significant success.

This is a very different starting place than the idealised strategy that can't go anywhere else, or the intellectually perfect strategy that cannot be executed. The latter starting points are no longer justifiable opening moves with clients who are looking to make their best brands work with discretionary audiences, more cost effectively. These same people are often in a hurry, working to a timetable set by others' deadlines, and of course they themselves are like users. They can only respond to clear stimuli.

Also for decades an old idea generation and execution model worked without too many challenges. A lead agency made things that helped creative people win awards they awarded each other. Brands would get more recognition, especially within the advertising industry. People would get promoted. In the 80's things began to move faster, expectations changed, and usurpers appeared. Clients were looking for short as well as long-term returns, as they managed their business and their careers in shorter and steeper upward spirals. The past was someone else's fault, and the future would be someone else's problem probably in about a year. Agency teams mirrored this. But clients were also developing stronger peripheral vision, and they began looking for solutions to old and fresh challenges in new places. The original core agency team began to be marginalized as clients sought for help in micro-organisms that would become the internet and the mobile phone, micro-payments and e-business, MP3's and multiple platforms. The original attractors were losing their lustre, and it showed, as they continued to offer up their worthy but superseded services. The way to survive was either to become a Supernova and buy up emerging talent to service new channel opportunities, or to be lean and independent specialists, who might become ripe for acquisition, or remain fiercely independent.

Meanwhile users were getting more sophisticated and less gullible about the methodologies selected to conduct a dialogue with them. Not every brand was being bought anymore because it said something about you. People continued to make decisions and choices for different reasons than those that marketing departments and research companies wanted or wished. In other words, the user was no longer playing the game in a passive way. Brands were increasingly elective and not default choices, and users mixed and matched them in ways manufacturers hadn't dreamed of doing, or couldn't control. Chavs and Burberry, text messaging, file sharing, brand abandoning, The Gap, M&S.

This is where different versions of reality came from.

Just as ideas can come from many places, the skill being in the ability to identify fruitful sources and nurture them, so brands can also be nurtured from surprising sources. The style of nurturing produces different results.

We have seen how the command and control models of brand management derived from religion and military codes, and permeated the understanding of brands and the style of presenting their propositions to users for years. This was one form of nurturing. A combination of the fragmentation of convenient typologies of users, like ABC1's, 17–25 year olds, etc., an improved understanding of the psychology of social relationships and interactions, and the choice of media distribution channels, has allowed us to recognise the depth and richness of individuals. But much behaviour in building connections with and between them has still lagged behind the potential for more fruitful forms of nurturing.

New questions are always being asked, and fear sometimes drives the line of questioning, but much of these new lines of inquiry have been in the wrong directions. The questions about what are the most appropriate media channels for user engagement in today's fragmented world should become easier when a brand and its roles have been identified with a clarity that suits both the moment and the sharper tools of identification for nurturing that are now available. Once these have also been analysed to compensate for the diffraction effects they can produce, the potential for brand nurturing with less waste becomes more realistic. This should be approached as a practical and productive piece of reduction, of simplification, not an excuse to generate higher and higher mounds of impenetrable intellectualisation, which can be a significant barrier to real progress.

So now we are back to this 'thing' called simplification.

Why should we bother? Two reasons,

1. Too many people are trying to put too many brands in one small area of space.

2. It is not realistic and affordable for many to try to be in that particular space any more.

The US comedian Steven Wright once said, "What's the point of having everything? Where would you put it?" We need new ways to release brands and their development and survival from closed spaces, or cul-de-sacs, where some of them are condemned or patronised for failing to live up to 'real proper brand' standards'.

Brands might be divided into categories like luxury, or premium supermarket own label, but today too many are expected to deliver a highly focused set of superior values – things that make 'brands' different from ordinary products. Brand differentiation usually involves an attempt to lift a product up and out of a merely functional area, and give it emotional or other value triggers, including a personality, all of which are meant to make it stand out from other brands and at the same time be even more palatable to users. Brands really are clustering in an increasingly cluttered space.

As we reviewed developments, we noted that in the old brand-building models, the user would be expected to have a dependent relationship on a brand, for life, rewarding the brand with levels of worship, tantamount to Blind Faith, and a desire to pass on the excellence of this state of affairs, or dependency, to others, non-users, or, worse, lapsed users. If the Brand wasn't being a sunbeam for Jesus, it was like a marriage, and the devil or divorce were not tolerable alternatives. Brands possessing these qualities, these virtues of dependence and obedience, were the ones to aspire to, by owners, those working on them, and by users.

It's not surprising that creative people, or those in creative organisations, have devoted so much time to elaborating the soft side of this equation, the faithful emotional bond, since it allows for more expression than simply focusing on the functionality of what they come to regard as being mundane products alone, and it elevates the involved into a place of higher purpose.

So we see brands becoming the 'Love Marks' or 'Passion Brands' of people who have spent a large part of their careers in advertising organisations, with eloquent rationales for those that can and should manifest these higher dimensions. How else are creative teams meant to be inspired? Until recently, once a communications company had written a strategy, and then a creative brief, it assumed total ownership of a brand's core communications, often telling the brand managers or owners that they couldn't change the creative product or perspective that had been developed, without dire consequences. Clients were often treated like the suggestible housewives they were both ultimately targeting.

"You know, we are the custodians of the brand. You are merely its manufacturers and distributors. Don't mess with us". And for ages the Mad Men got away with it.

This was always rather charming, given the presumption of excellence based on entirely subjective criteria or admirable rhetoric, and no evidence of a thorough contextual analysis of a brand's position and performance. That would simply get in the way of the superior judgement of the creatives and the omniscient suits. Talk about high priests of communication. Those who stood up for their own brands stood a chance of being excommunicated by The Agency. These people would have to leave the blessed sphere and instead make their fortune making silicon chips and aircraft landing gear, away from the judging eyes of the Brand Masters. This is not made up.

So what you often ended up with in these scenarios was a brand or category drive towards a kind of functional and emotional nirvana, or heaven, and an almighty push for all follower brands to occupy it. Brands that couldn't possess these extra dimensions would not be worked on by the higher-ups, or were condemned to be addressed by low-life communications i.e. not award-winning communications, developed by low-lifes, i.e. not award-winning talent. People in communication companies of this sort were like moths to a flame, trying their best to get near to the source of the light of high status brands and high status creative awards, basking in the warmth of the glow. It worked for large numbers of now comfortable retirees.

"I managed these brands. Look at me". Not for them the toil of working on household   products, which was often where the real revenue that funded other indulgences came from, but the promise of fame through fashion, or other 'added-value' brands. And in brand-owning companies there was the same pressure to handle or be associated with sweet-spot brands. Once this was also the case in those companies specialising in cleansing products with hero brands that conferred status on their managers, a bit like those 'Best Public Toilets in the City' surveys metropolitan magazines put out from time to time.

So if you're brand wasn't in the sweet spot, you weren't (either) a hero – sorry, no promotion, no raise, no bonus, no chance. When the Boston Consulting Group (BCG) first produced its famous grid:

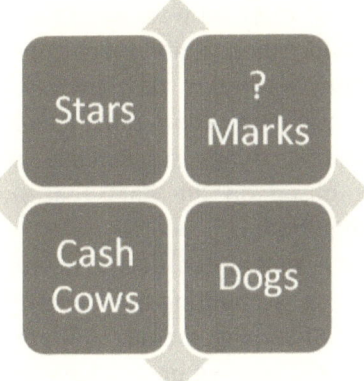

people did the 'piranhas on the dead sheep' trick. Here was a way to classify portfolios of products and understand where the real profit opportunities lay. This was portfolio matrix theory. Clients would construct a revenue-based model, and communications agency creative people would construct an awards-based model.

In enlightened companies, people were moved around the organisation so they could experience what it was like to work on products that were in each quadrant, with their own distinctive challenges. Yet that word 'star' still carried an awful lot of the wrong kind of clout. It can be easy to be blinded by the model, such that it is leading the analysis of where to go, rather than reflecting it.

The problem with this grid was in the way the matrix was applied. One piece of research showed how two professors conducted a five year long test on an investment decision, for over 1000 students in management programmes at universities around the world, with over half among MBA's with at least two years business experience. The professors asked the students to select one of two different investment opportunities – one firm that was obviously profitable and one that was not, only they labelled the profitable firm a dog, and the unprofitable one a star. The description contained sufficient information so that the profit maximising decision was obvious. The issue was, would the subjects apply the BCG matrix blindly? The answer? Many did. In fact, depending on whether they were in a control group or not, between 45% and 87% of the students selected the unprofitable choice that had been labelled a star. So the use of the famous model interfered with profit maximising. It provided a distorting lens for the incautious.

But the extensive life of the Grid was probably significantly driven by the fact that CEOs and other senior management could use the matrix to justify steps they wanted to take anyway. Its attractiveness was in its power as a communication tool. Its danger was that it enabled people to position things subjectively without exercising judgement and insight based on the data that was clearly in the shadow of this maximising model.

Where we go with our model can overcome this. It requires the application of clear thinking, accounting for the dangers of diffraction. Manipulated or purely self-serving models will not enhance market performance for long. This is why we do not have a 'best quadrant' in the model.

In another example, groups of people were asked to estimate a company's future sales and earnings per share based on a set of financial data. Afterwards, the professor told some of the groups they had performed well, and others they had performed poorly – but he did this at random. In fact the high and the low performing groups had done equally well. The only difference was what the professor had told them. He then asked the groups to rate their performance on a range of issues. The results? When told they had performed well people described their groups as having been highly cohesive, with better communication, more openness to change, and superior motivation. When told they had performed poorly, people recalled a lack of cohesion, poor communication, and low motivation. The conclusion was that people attribute one set of characteristics to those groups they believe are effective, and a very different set of characteristics to groups they believe are ineffective. If you are in an organisation like this, you'd better be in the Star System.

One seasoned Board Director of a communications agency, a former client, asked why he was never invited to the parties that either celebrated small new business wins, or compensated losses. "Why do you ask?" the Chairman responded. "Because without the huge business I run that none of you want to go near, none of this would be possible". It didn't earn him any new party invites any time soon.

Managing brands is obviously made more challenging by the presence of these kinds of conflicting dynamics. People want signs, points of direction, disciplined focus, so they can distil a brand's 'essence'. Yet they also revel in the sheer complexity of it all. "There is nothing more empowering than believing you know a complicated secret, especially where complexity adds a heavy layer of mystique to the process". It's an Alchemical Corporation.

We have already seen numerous approaches to capturing a brand's core meaning. Often, after days or months of work, a brand is triumphantly summed up in a statement of four or five words - max. Remember "Coke is it". It has been compressed and compacted into an orb of explosive potential. However, this statement is not the sole star. It is often at the centre of a galaxy of other words or phrases, clustered all around. These are meant to represent variations in brand values or personality or capabilities. Often these additional words are there to indicate that a number of corporate departments or other stakeholders involved in the project were actually listened to. We have seen such charts bearing 100 words or more. Trouble is, every time a distilled statement about the brand is produced, twenty eight people reject it because it doesn't contain their words.

There was a time when one client had a strategy page that always asked for a 'key consumer benefit'. This was supposed to be the pure statement of what would eventually become an advertising selling proposition, or, what users call a slogan. It often took months for people to debate what the words should be, even though no-one outside a small group would ever see them. Finally, when advertising ideas were produced, the copy was always rejected because it didn't say exactly what the key consumer benefit said, even though this was a piece of cold prose. Incidentally, no benefit could be written that didn't include the words 'great taste' either. What else should a food product be? Oh, sorry, 'New Improved Great Taste.'

That is why 'beautifully engineered' keeps appearing on this kind of chart. In the case of one car manufacturer, their four word core brand statement was surrounded by no less than 98 qualifiers, all of which were supposed to be reflected in core communications. Any evidence showing that the qualifiers had been ignored and once again any communications proposals were rejected by departmental owners of the corporate 'solar system' and any of its qualifiers, instantly. This approach captured everything and enabled the delivery of nothing. These are what we call prime examples of the practising of a fetish for complexity. You certainly could not deliver solutions in a 30 second long commercial, and that's in the days when 'solutions' hadn't become the answer to everything. And on a poster – forget it. Sadly, all too often the required sense of humour and confidence to break down these costly time-wasting pursuits was nowhere to be seen. Just too much time and money and resource had been thrown at them, so they had to work. The best examples of emperor's new clothes spotting were left to ordinary Joes on the street that enjoyed playing with the conceit. "Liquid Transfer Solutions" was the great promise we saw on the back of a van that belonged to a company selling garden hoses.

You can put loads on the internet of course, but don't expect everyone to look at it in all its detail. There are rules of engagement there too.

"We believe that the more information we have, the more accurate our decisions will be". Empirical evidence does not support such a belief. Instead, more information merely seems to increase our confidence that we are right without necessarily improving the accuracy of our decisions.

These are some of the barriers to simplicity we have encountered, and still do, every day, in trying to build brands effectively.

How can we help brands, their owners, and their users, better here?

Let's take some simple empirical steps forward.

First, we re-acknowledge that our life experience tells us not all brands are the same, or all share similar properties. If we can accept that, then maybe we can liberate some brands from an overcrowded space and in the rapidly expanding resulting universe, we can observe many different kinds of brands, yet still have a measure of meaningful groupings. Just as in astronomy, with its classifications of galaxies and stars, young and old, separating and colliding, brands can be big or small, being born or be dying, shining bright or disappearing into black holes of obsolescence, and so on. So instead of trying to find 'A General Unified Theory of Everything', let's start with saying – brands are different. They don't have to be embraced or unified in one collective definition, because brands aren't all the same anymore. Maybe once upon a time it was possible to homogenise the way we talked about them, the way we chose to present them to our fellow friends as 'customers' or 'users'. But it simply does not make sense anymore. You only have to think about your own experience. What happens every day? Let's remind ourselves again, do you really think about a box of cornflakes with the same intensity with which you regard your beloved Diesel jeans, or a long-desired Porsche car? Of course you don't. That only happens in advertising.

So how come we expect other people to? How come we go along with the notion that women might choose a brand of fabric conditioner because it allows their kids to experience 'the essence of love' when they are away from home, or that using one brand of packet soup mix is going to make you a better Mum in the eyes of others? We look back on the advertising of 50 years ago and laugh at the way in which women and Mums in particular, were depicted, occupying their rightful place in a patriarchal world. But take a good look around, and you'll see that not much has really changed in terms of how we try to attract people's attention to our brand or service.

But in reality, the way in which we interact with brands has changed enormously.

Google is on every list of the world's Top Ten brands. It is useful, and for some, difficult to imagine living without. It makes life easier. But do you have an emotional relationship with it? Of course you don't, unless you work there. Why should you?

You will either be feeling a great sense of relief at this moment, or a sense of anger that we are opting out of the challenge of 'complexity' the business has elected to develop. We would say that too many people are still looking in the wrong places to collectively define brands.

Some would argue that these days, "Brands have become ends in themselves, as opposed to a means to an end". It is currently fashionable to posit the belief that the way forward is product + brand + experience characterised by context. So a product is what it does, a brand is how it makes you feel, and an experience is how it fits in your life. We use products, we buy brands, but we live experiences." [2]

This kind of approach still leads people to the view that a highly engaging context needs to be created for you to value a brand. This leads to more significant time and resource being wasted. Some brands might have excited you once, some still do, but many don't, and shouldn't. They're no longer in the excitement business. Should they be demoted from brand status? No.

Brands have measurable lives, not necessarily predictably measurable lives, and life stages. Essentially they are born (created) and gain recognition. Some then gain fame or notoriety, one version of which is celebrity, some gain respect. For others there is a long process of maturation, familiarisation and then slow decline or stabilisation, and a brand becomes part of the general galaxies of the Universal Market. Some brands might have a spectacular late period of brightness before they too expend their energy or are consumed by others. That's the Big Picture. But of course, within this perspective, many variations are possible, and can be witnessed. Investment in communications for a brand, then, is a function of the extent to which, beyond profit generation, you want to drive recognition, fame, respect, recurring brightness, and residual memories, which may have a beneficial effect on other brands in a portfolio, or on brand owners, or users.

Not every brand needs to go along a narrow linear path. Recognition-to-respect may be best for some brands, without the starbursts of fame or celebrity. Recognition may not need to be universal. Bentley cars, now owned by Volkswagen, sold its Continental version in Australia for a modest £120.000. Bentley said it didn't have to do any traditional advertising. A spokeswoman for the brand said, "Those who can afford the cars will find us." This is true for some even in a recessionary environment. Some brands may be most desirable, with a very short afterlife. Occasionally, when we are not swept up in the rush of responses for our time in eight places at once, and our second assistant is just about managing our third iPhone in a row, we step back and like some late night student moment of awakening, slur:

What are brands for today?

A look at too many narratives might lead you to produce one of those 'numbers' books that sit in the business book sections at airports, you know, the '42 most effective ways to achieve 'x'' books. Our version, if we had been forced to produce one of these variants today, could have been called "The 7 Wonders of Brands". In this world, brands:

- save your life (keep you out of trouble)

- make you feel good

- make you look good

- enable you to have better relationships

- take you to another space

- keep you in line

- any combination of the above i.e. Brand Y does this and this.

So, we would have produced something formulaic to fit the demands of the market, but we wouldn't have been able to endorse the message in the content. It would have been a triumph of form over substance. As usual, it seems with brands, this kind of narrative would have just led us back to the routes that tend to make too many want to occupy one special place or territory in what actually should be a universe of possibilities. Times are moving on. We need something else to capture what we understand about the new perspectives we have gained.

It's like with Kodak again, in the old days. There is a world where anger, frustration, jealousy, tantrums, sadness and other emotions and behaviour all have their recognisable place in the Wheel of Life. You might say yourself, as Kodak did, that most of that's for the photojournalists, preferably in black and white, and in old magazines or art galleries. The marketing department, who lived in a world of colour and light, albeit in a factory in Rochester, NY, continued to put the brand in a box called birthday, wedding, party, as if the world only knew how to smile. But as we all know these days, there is a range of needs, wants, expressions, feelings, and interpretations that make us the generally accepted beings we are. In this reality, as opposed to in fictional narratives, brands need to have those wholes recognised. Funnily enough, Kodak itself celebrated emotional variety in its corporate cinema ads, where it spoke of its contribution to cinematographers, but that's probably a bit kind of arty and indulgent, you know?

You can talk about 'want' brands and 'need' brands, as we do.[9] And this at least has the virtue of recognising that people might after all have different relationships with brands. . Communication cynics point out that many users don't know what they want or need, and that their views change all the time anyway. But that's the point. That's the way it is. A bicycle tyre pump may be boring but it's not useless. It's basically a need product. For some people, if it functions well and is called a 'Canondale' pump, or a 'Giant' pump, its functionality may be accorded a higher status depending on your feelings about the over-riding brand name, and with a premium price to match, but it is still, for most, fundamentally a need product orbiting in a need territory. It may even have helped save your life, in one of the narrative worlds defined above. If it has played an emotional role, it may be because it helped you get your bike's tyres blown up so you could ride faster to your friend's party. That probably still doesn't make it the dominant brand in your life today. What's wrong with that? Nothing.

Here are some branded products that played a role in your life this weekend, maybe: toilet tissue, wiping cloths, washing up liquid, towels, milk, batteries, keys, credit cards, plastic bags. Over time, brands in many categories like the ones these products could be classified in may have tried to wrap themselves up in narratives that try to give them almost superpower status. These have included those brands that were fuelled by expensive short-term communication wars between share hungry manufacturers, ranging from lawn mower makers to car tyres. They all created self-fulfilling narrative codes and did their best to get you to 'emotionalise' with them.

Now, a good communications expert could have talked for months about the insights that would create new market opportunities for, say, Swan Vesta matches, if there was a client brief and potentially significant revenue to attract management attention.

"It's not any old match you know – it comes from green Scandinavian forests, its light is consistent, its burn rate steady and long, its ease of self-driven combustion reliable even in damp conditions. Yes, indeed, it is *The Light of My Life*".

In fact, a Swan Vesta appears to be a perfectly reasonable match. Respectable. Functional. Fire-creating. That's it. Once upon a time it may have had a competitive edge, when all around it were cheap wood-splitting damp-prone finger-nail biting breaking un-lightable bits of East European communist wood. But we no longer need our matches to be served up with stories. Some people probably don't even see a match from one month to another.

That's very true for a lot of brands we used to clump under the umbrella of fast moving consumer goods. Age has made them slightly wearier.

Some older readers or historians may want to recall the money and content devoted to telling you on television what was the best bird-seed for your budgerigar –'Trill', anyone?' You will still find it on many a supermarket gondola, reflecting on its former status as a brand worthy of being aspired to serve upon. It may come with English and Turkish on the label, a clue to where business is still prevalent. Many primarily functional products have tried to get front of stage to say, brazenly, "If you don't pay attention, and do what we say, and do it our way, you will have let me down, you will have let yourself down, and you will have let the whole house down, not to mention Joey", Joey of course being the pet budgie.

This is where we want to sit down, have a coffee, and after a while, say,

Products whose functionality is clear should get on with communicating their functional advantages, or nothing.

Today we live in a changed and still changing world, and in many markets we don't want or need dependent relationships with brands.

In the old days, you wouldn't be able to go out if you hadn't scrubbed the floors clean. That was the basic message behind an ad that said you can get that job done quicker and easier with Johnson Wax. This spin on the Cinderella story was, surprise, surprise, aimed at women in the US in the 20th century. More than that, this particular product was positioned as the way to preserve your youth and beauty. Less than 100 years ago the home was a very dangerous place where marriages could easily fall apart, triggered by the wrong purchase of a stock-cube, coffee, or detergent. These days the 'mocking grounds' have moved on, and you are less likely to be spanked for choosing the wrong coffee in the supermarket.[3]

Products whose functionality is clear should get on with communicating their functional advantages, or nothing.

Today we live in a changed and still changing world, and in many markets we don't want or need dependent relationships with brands.

---

11. Language and Structure – New Perspectives

The 'thing' communications companies pride themselves on delivering these days has been finessed to define a higher level of competence and rarity – ideas. This is both less tangible than specific execution or medium-based products or services, and more flexible. This approach can also command a premium in the hands of negotiators who are now much less frightened than they once were about big consulting operations eating their lunch. But one of the challenges for idea-generating companies must be to agree on the form of the ideas they sell. In the old days a big portion of these for the advertising agencies was simply television commercials and press ads. No more. The search for new ideas opens the box again on some fascinating areas about where ideas might come from, how they get harnessed, and who owns or judges them. We are back in a world of perspectives and contexts, power and control.

What processes are used today to get an idea about something, inside these organisations? What should briefs look like? Where do insights come from? Players today are struggling to get the best fit between their ideas, concepts and the executions of them. Language is used not only to define the products of our ideas, but also to define the boundaries in which they exist.

We will now revisit some controversial places and topics we need to examine before the final piece of practical input can best be presented. Since language is about helping us to structure our lives and classify things, we need to be acutely aware of its power in helping to both construct and create changes in the context of the ways we work, and the places we work in.

Many of us have experienced and learned the variant languages that corporations we work in or with develop, from pro to anti jargon, from a fondness for acronyms and abbreviations, to a desire for clarity in a certain style, from the defensiveness of bureaucratic descriptions to the sound-bites on news items. Some styles we like, some we detest. It often depends on whether we are message producers or receivers. Messages are like brands. Their reception depends on the context of how we transmit and receive them, and perspective and interpretation play their role. In that regard, brands themselves are merely codes of information strung together. What brings them to life are the bases of information we each individually possess, and the means to asses them relative to all the other information we have processed. Bits of language not only conjoin and divide us numerically, they also work on us at other levels, helping us form the basis of powerful commercial relationships, whether they are of the brand user variety or the career-building variety.

Brands and their chosen language are these days constructed to get the best response they can to their overall message, and the smart ones have multiple messages.

Brand and business developers are increasingly focused on how language can address the challenge of generating further revenue from the 'intellectual property' we are seeking to develop to enhance our business and reputation. The growth of the intellectual property business in the last twenty years has been phenomenal, and within that such specialist areas as image rights management for sports, music, and film stars have grown astronomically. Interestingly, some of those who have gained most from this development have been the flexible and chameleonic characters who can change their 'look' quickly to meet shifting circumstances and desires. Some others have been able to capitalise on a more focused iconic status, but few remain embedded in a bit of stubborn concrete, unmoving, and survive. Avoiding the ability to evolve will ultimately be more dangerous than facing up to it. If we don't know how language helps protect our intellectual capital, or keep it tethered, we risk squandering our core values, and the currencies we use to trade our values. Language can be used to define differences, but also it can be used to define commodities. Commoditisation is dangerous for those who believe they can escape its pull without effort.

For those of an academic bent who enjoyed the spread of post-modern French intellectual thinking, views on language and perception gave us some wonderfully convoluted and juicy thoughts. As any old Monsieur Semiotician would tell us, a name is not only a sign itself, but also a signifier of a set of meanings associated with the sign. This is as true of descriptors like 'Managing Director' as of brands, and of associates, or executives, or vice presidents, as of products, and categories, and markets.

Here's another way of looking at it. The day the mail or the call comes to tell you you've got the new job, it usually also defines the role and gives you a title, often eliciting feelings of pride, excitement, and potential. The same title, when exposed to industry veterans, may elicit hoots of derision, from people who either know the job description is inflated, or think they are in significantly superior positions. At one stage in life you're a student, the next you're a graduate, then you're an 'executive', and so on. Of course, how people feel about this too depends on their perspective. Some would like to go straight to being 'The One', and unless they set up their own operation, they will usually defer the title option for a few months.

New titles and roles can have profound effects, irrespective of the personalities of those with the actual titles. Take planners, those sought-after thinkers first nurtured into being by Stanley Pollitt and Stephen King. They were a new breed half a century ago. They provided a form of discontinuity, a process of disruption we know creates periodic desirable waves in enterprises, and they went on to create a potent level of demand from clients keen to capitalise on the new currency. Planners were what the enlightened wanted for Christmas.

Fifty years later, which isn't actually a bad run, the currency in some quarters is a tad tarnished, but there were lots of different kinds of planners in circulation, with different values and weights. Planners started out as competitive differentiators, and those having them had an edge for certain clients. It was all presented in a pioneering spirit, the bringing to life of new insights about the way users behaved and the ways communications worked. Planning was credible to those who wanted to be at the cutting edge. As the role spread, the value of planning and planners changed. Meanings multiplied. Challengers came to question the role. Planners started to build worlds within worlds and take on the roles of departments, defending territories and building relationships that had little to do with their original purpose. They started to demand ownership of key things, like 'insight', and some expected others to serve their needs like so many drones. Even fewer people were allowed to have ideas without an appropriate title. Clever ones declared they had no vested interests. Many were really clever. Not quite so many had no vested interests at all.

Then clients began to re-take ownership of insights, or proprietary information, as they invested in ways to enhance their understanding of the people who kept them in business, their users. Suspicions about agencies' ability to give objective advice based on deep understanding were fuelled by realisations that many agency suppliers were also desperately trying to protect easy revenue sources that were also coming under scrutiny. Ownership of a then often ill-defined intellectual property was slowly shifting.

At the same time, as business became more and more global, managers in different cultures were realising that they applied different values to organisation responsibilities and practices. Cultures are perceived not only in terms of shared values, but of choices between values, according to where people are working. So culture includes value systems. Planning wasn't always the flavour of the month when it tried to travel from its very western sources.

The culture of a geographically bound group plays a significant role in how its members perceive the world and solve problems, so actions and recommendations may seem logical to the proposing group but illogical and sometimes perverse to the observing or receiving group. All this has a major impact on sprawling organisations' abilities to change quickly. It may go some way to explaining why so many international companies remain networked local tribes rather than seamlessly integrated multinational clusters.

This should make us more aware of the need to understand these kinds of cultural and contextual gravitational pull effects on people, but deadlines and other pressures often force these issues out of the arena of understanding. No-one is prepared to stand back. Shifting sources of solutions become fashionable. For a while it was all about getting a few Brits in to shake things all about. Then it was the turn of the Antipodeans. Then it was the turn of entrepreneurial South Americans, and so on. All this has equally profound effects on helping to source, manage, and motivate people, and of course on all the ideas that surface that could provide profitable solutions to challenges. Within this shifting world of solution sourcing, people who are ostracised from the idea generating process will ultimately withhold their ideas and then take them elsewhere. This can have profound consequences on the bottom-line, and the overall business.

Depending on your operating culture, what you are called within this overall environment, and what you are invited to contribute remain significant in ways you might forget as you hurtle upwards in your corporate career trajectory. Many not in the know would feel there wasn't a great deal of difference between, say, calling someone a test pilot, and calling them an astronaut. But this bugged Chuck

Yeager, the real person and hero of Tom Wolfe's *The Right Stuff*, all his life. One of the world's greatest test pilots, who enabled the US astronaut and space exploration programme to succeed, he never got to be called an astronaut, and neither did he get the package that went with it. He was not too happy. Do you care? That probably depends on who you are and where you come from.

When was the last time someone introduced a client to you as "Mr/Ms X, VP of Alpha Corp" to have them add, "Senior VP, actually"? In the US, titles are defined by law. So before you next rush to describe yourself as Worldwide President, check it out. One person in our circle suffered after describing their visitor as "Creative Director, New York", to be instantly castigated through the correction, "That's Creative Director, New York and Northern Hemisphere". Still, there were always two senior client titles we coveted. One was at Heinz, where we felt 'Head of Tomatoes' probably carried a lot of significance, and the other was for an atomic clocks co-ordinator at Hewlett-Packard, who had managed to get the title 'Head of Time' on his card.

If you're still not sure any of this has any impact, today's current insulting phrase doing the rounds of US movies is the "That's way above your pay grade," put-down. Hurting yet?

There is a need to reconsider how to get the most out of more people who have the potential to make a contribution, wherever they are in the organisation, or in its distributed sphere of influence.

Look at it this way.

The old-style structure model for many companies would have looked like this, and in this world, the Boss would sit at the top of the hierarchy in terms of deciding what's good, what's creative, and what's right for the brand in terms of its communications ideas.

Communications Organisation Management Structure

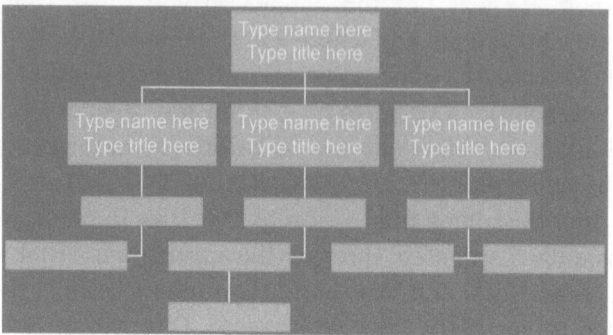

Perhaps it is time to reconsider this, and look at working structure models where other skills and talents are brought to bear on defining and developing creativity and brand-building solutions.

The new world model might look like this:

The Intellectual Property Organisation Asset Management Structure

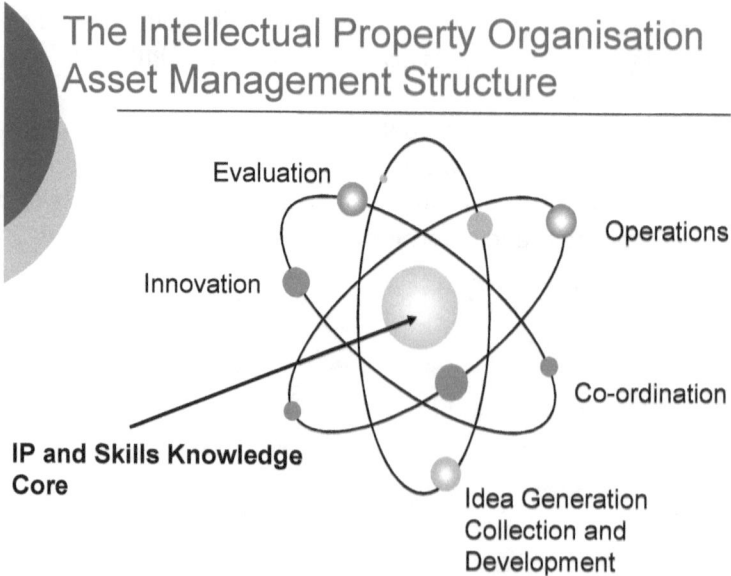

Much of the thinking, creativity and innovation in a company may never see the light of day. It remains tacit in the minds of frustrated competent people. And they're not all in departments with the words 'creative' or 'innovation', or 'development' in them. "It's all very well to talk about open networks, but who calls the tune?" ask the heads of department. "What's wrong with the way we are?"

Nothing, as long as we accept that the former kinds of structure look back on the ways services used to be described and provided. If you keep on going the way you are, you will miss the road to the future. A shift in perspective needs to be applied to help focus on how to do two things:

Break down burdensome structures.

Find ways to get more useable ideas from existing but under-utilised or under-recognised resources.

At 3M, it used to be the case that a substantial portion of people's time was made free to pursue innovation projects, and up to 35% of the company's business each year came from new business. In white goods and hardware companies, advances are being made by changing the way people's ideas can be harnessed. Haier, a major refrigeration provider, along with other things, competes not just on cost, but also on quality and innovation, like with small electric wine cellars and mini-fridges. In this organisation it is mandatory for employees to conceive of innovative ideas and insights. Google gives a number of its people one day a week to work on whatever projects stimulate them.

Idea generation should not be restricted to a structure worthy of the last century, but should be the property of most, if not the whole organisation. These days there are means to test ways forward without having to commit the whole company first. When the whole company is committed, hearts and minds will be surprisingly more engaged.

Without looking at the ways language informs culture and consequently structure, the ways in which ideas are shaped may not be open to reaching their greatest potential. Ideas will be diluted through language, titles, roles and controls that, like the past, will be another country. We know they do things differently there.

We are now ready to show how our approach can work, simply and practically.

> **More people have creative potential than is generally acknowledged. It's natural.**
>
> **What we have to do is get better at harnessing it.**

12. Co-ignition – Getting More with Less.

We have looked at several ways of simplifying things, from ways of thinking about brands and communications, research and planning, organisation, structure, and language. We have looked at the ways in which people connect, at models of command and control, at the influences of culture and behaviour on attitudes towards managing brands, and emerging user behaviour. We have also looked at a series of barriers to progress that continue to spring up in different guises every day. Now it is time to pull together our distillations and devices and pose the really practical question:

How do we put our approach to work in practice? [1]

Challenges and changes are the name of the game. There is often still a real gap between noticing change and adapting behaviour at the point where we move from brand user world to the corporate world. "OK, so things are changing out there, but they're not changing in here". For example, as individuals compose their identities, they are also free to choose multiple allegiances for the first time in history. Previously "the self was bounded by birth, location, occupation and social class...For most of history, to know yourself was in large part simply to know your place." [2] That is still true in big parts of the globe and big parts of the corporate world today. The conflict continues, and while some continue to analyse it, others capitalise on it. Today it appears that people are still willing to pay for brand names and designer labels out of all proportion to their actual value. [3]

Value is now a subjective proposition, like authenticity.

Look at how rarity continues to command a premium, from football shirts to Ferraris. In this world, we are not going to see a balanced value equation everywhere between brand managers and users any time soon. In Me World [4], and the world of *The Brand and I*, it is further pointed out that for many, "any limit we experience, even a logical one, on what might be possible, we now interpret as an unjustifiable imposition on our freedom and expertise". This world-view reflects our tastes and judgements back on ourselves, so we all create our own individual realities. From behind the old-fashioned battlements of these realities we are often caught claiming that we are too busy to reconsider and re-shape views or perspectives.

Focus is lost, and issues multiply as a consequence of our multiplying interests and identities, built into ever more busy contexts. Everyone is a multiplayer today, not just a passive observer. How things have changed over a hundred years or so: "What is this life, if, full of care, we have no time to stand and stare?" [5] Pressure on time means we now have people classifying time as me-time, quality time, real-time. It is harder to capture the resource called attention.

Brands increasingly strive to claim authenticity as a reason for consideration. Often they do this in precisely the wrong way by constantly chanting how 'real' they are, how genuine they are. [6] They clamour for a place of honour in our fragmented catalogue of time. They do not understand that transparency is stronger than claims of authenticity today And we use a multiplicity of means to splice time and protect our own 'real' and multiple identities: TV digital boxes, voice-mail, on-line personalities, all filtering and layering availability and presence. But we can't pay attention to everything at the same time. It was the physicist Wheeler who said "Time is nature's way of stopping everything happening at once". Managers continue to try to defy nature's givens, wanting their brands to magically overcome barriers and filters, because they're really real. As one of the author of *Mediated* friends said, "What's so great about reality?"

This isn't a philosophy book, but we do have to come to terms with the fact that one of the challenges of "I am" is that although we have the notion we are a single unique being, we also know we have multiple selves that shift with contexts. We have oceans of personality. So a brand is either lacking in personality by being too focused, or it too must have multiple meanings according to users' perspectives and relationships with it.

Who then is doing the talking, and who is doing the listening? If we accept the principle that we cannot encode everything that is going on around us at the same time, we have to accept that we make selections based on what we perceive to be important, and switch off to the rest. Yet many companies still behave as though this can be totally overcome. *The Brand and I* is as much a statement about a desire for control as it is a reflection of the subjectivity applied to shaping brand destinies.

Let's see how these kinds of issues can be managed in organisations today. While we may be uniquely multiple, we still share certain characteristics, and these include the ability to be creative, innovative, and nurturing, to different degrees. An organisation is not only expected to develop plans to make itself different, better is different, it is also expected to execute its strategy by mobilising its resources. Strategy involves risk because it forces us to make choices, and we can never know how things might turn out all the time. Going to market also involves further risk because it means deciding which limited elements will be most effective in fulfilling the strategy in a given timeframe, and against competitors.

People manage and handle risk differently, so teams have to be varied to move from strategy development to going to market. What may come as a surprise is that at the strategy phase of development, a loose and open approach to strategy generation, and then a more focused approach to turning ideas into products and services, may well be the best use of resources. Over-cohesive groups with a totally shared sense of identity at the beginning of the development will often under-utilise information, and censor those who offer competing views. [7]

Current moderation techniques focus on positivity. 'How to' is a common theme that can make it difficult to talk about ideas outside of accepted wisdom. So groups are bound and exhorted to find positive things to say about whatever brand is under consideration, even very old ones that are no longer shining stars, which of course makes it difficult to view a brand in the way a consumer might. One of us, attending a brand vision exercise for a famous but old food brand, was asked to consider what consumers might write as an epitaph if the brand were dead. Even in this type of projective exercise it can be difficult to tell the truth, simply. In reality the answer might be "Nothing – I don't care". Confronted with 20 senior executives in a brand visioning exercise, who all understood it would be politically unacceptable to make negative comments about their most recently acquired brand, it was not easy, but at least the 'epitaph' exercise enabled the introduction of some realism into the discussion. And that is what we believe we must strive for.

The basic goal at the first stage of strategy development is to identify and nurture opportunity, promote creativity, and improve the quality and taking of decisions. This means having to create scenarios that will increase the chances of people feeling comfortable they can disclose what they know. Remember that in the new mediated world we live in, we are tempted to seek out the information that mirrors back our own biases, opinions and perspectives, and conforms to our naturally distorted views of reality. This requires skilful facilitation to harness workable solutions.

And that also means enabling a discussion of potential issues or negatives, rather than simply facilitating the creation of a brand universe that will never exist anywhere except in a brand manager's head.

Practically, one of the things we do in co-igniting these developments is to help people sharpen their insights and perspectives. We run one exercise where all get to map product categories on our quadrant model. Brand orbits are then drawn in. Everyone gets the opportunity to see simply and clearly the impact of different perspectives. Different parties e.g. brand owner, user, trade partner, etc. often have varied views on the brands, which categories and quadrants they might feasibly sit in, and what the shape of their orbits might be. This is a simple way to establish where gaps exist, where differences need to be highlighted or addressed, and where action might be required to shift perspectives. It is just as important to manage the process of killing off routes with no real future, which means having positive views and managing practices in how to deal with 'losing'. 'Fast failure' is General Electric's way of accepting that failure is an integral part of trying to be innovative. Learning how to judge what innovation to kill means we have to place more trust and authority in the management of and culture in the organisation. This is also where a brand user may very well not be right in helping with innovation, depending on the category being looked at. This is a daunting challenge for some. In *The Culture of the Amateur* [8], it is pointed out that "the common community is shattering into 300,000 personalised points of view" and someone is going to have to exercise some authority and responsibility in deciding how to handle these emerging and often poorly informed masses when it comes to trying out new products and services with them.

In the second phase, going to market, although great rigour is required in deselecting or rejecting ideas that will needlessly tie up funds and time, at the very beginning of an idea generation process, involvement again can be broadened. Among others [9], commentators on branding governance make the point that imagination is a fundamental part of being human. More people than you imagine can make positive contributions to this stage of development.

All this accords entirely with our basic tenet that: Subjectivity in creating the destinies of many brands needs to be acknowledged and managed differently to improve value.

How this is manifested is clearly contextually bound by organisational culture and its defining operating language and structure. Generally speaking, where extended and greater levels of involvement and boundary breaking can be achieved, improved levels of effectiveness can occur. [10]

Managing this approach requires dexterous facilitation, especially where a high number of stakeholders with strong perspectives and views are involved. These people often want to modify everything to the point where only they can solve the problem. Sadly, management may find itself faced with a multiplicity of problems that can only be solved by such a King of the Castle. It is not easy to steer a steady course towards 'fit for purpose' solutions on this basis. It can be even harder in highly charged creative environments. This seeming contrariness arises because such companies often attract and succour people who run their own lives in highly controlled ways, and they are often very resistant to the same kinds of acts of 'disruption' they advocate for others. Even when things go right, it is still difficult, because of the influence of the Halo Effect. [11]

The people you choose to work with may radically change their views according to criteria they attribute to your performance that you can do little to control directly. Look briefly at an example from an organisation, rather than an individual – Cisco Systems. Way back in May 2000 this company was considered one of America's truly outstanding companies, in the same league as Intel, WalMart and General Electric, being voted number two behind GE by *Fortune* magazine in its annual polls of most admired companies. In May 2001 *Fortune* then said all that had made it great was false. No-one said that Cisco's culture had changed between 2000 and 2001, it was just that now, in retrospect, Cisco was described through a different lens – one of falling performance, and attributions get based on performance.

Distortion requires careful handling. Customers and brand users are not always seeing through clear lenses. You end up singing along with Carlos Santana "I ain't got nobody that I can depend on." This applied equally well within the Kodak organisation, where a degree of internal politics and a fear of the future blinkered the corporation into not seeing the reality and impact of the arrival and growth of digital photography. The quantity of data available to see a big picture is entirely irrelevant if the quality of its interpretation is poor, or deliberately biased in the service of another agenda. We also see that in a wide range of industries successful companies are repeatedly dislodged by new players because they were doing everything right. They focused on customer needs and invented things for them that looked right, failing to see how disruptive technologies were being created, and the speed at which their former loyalists were prepared to vote with their credit cards for the new upstarts. [12]

What drives brands are the perceptions of all the people involved in them. Job one is to pursue clarity of vision, to see clearly.

Clarity of vision also helps us see that brands don't all have to be defined in terms of the value of 'an experience' you have with them, or the amount of love and passion they can create. As Charles Handy reputedly pointed out in a presentation to an advertising agency, the very type of place many communications agencies are attracts very bright people who need to intellectualise what they are doing as part of their motivational belief/reward system. So it's not surprising those people don't crowd towards brands they don't find exciting, and wouldn't want to mention in media watering-holes. Just because some people don't get excited doesn't mean others can't be passionate about the products they handle. We would imagine people like the CEO of Reckitt Benckiser is justifiably excited and not too shy talking about household products which net the company enviable performance figures. It takes all sorts. The challenge is to translate passion, commitment and subjectivity into action users will respond to realistically, not to transform brand management blind or fanatical faith into gods and icons that will no longer be worshipped. There is a difference today between faith and respect.

Here is another case of perspective and insight turning into profitable action. The retractable landing gear of aircraft inspired the commercial pilot, a Mr McLaren, who used to watch his usually female passengers struggling to fold the old-fashioned prams and pushchairs they were trying to drag up his plane's steps, to design the kind of child buggy we now all take for granted. It's a different way of seeing things, a different mind-set. Not every brand needs to discover a 'lost passion' or 'love', and communicate this with its customers. Those who want to will find like-minded souls to do the job, but to say a brand just isn't a brand without all these emotionally engaging extras is too narrowcast. Relevant functionality is highly valuable. And value is not always about addition. Look at WalMart and South Western Airlines, or Accor Hotels. You can always find someone who will have a professed or real deep emotional relationship with something you wouldn't look at twice, even something branded, but that doesn't mean the brand is suddenly transposed to a place with a high level of emotional content for the rest of us. The world has an enormous spectrum of tastes. For certain brands you might consider someone's relationship with it to be almost a fetish, but for many people, and brands, they just don't go that far, and they are certainly not queuing up to have passionate love affairs with disposable nappies and head-over-heels-in love new mothers, however the research is interpreted.

We return to one of our core themes. Many brands simply function well, consistently, reliably, quietly, every day. A lot of brands just don't need to go back to their points of creation in the history of the universe, because the path researched may no longer help beat or point to the path forward. Heritage helps for some brands, but for others it's just a waste of time, except for those being rewarded as archivists. These brands just aren't crying out for longevity – Space Dust, Mutant Ninja Turtles, New Coke anyone?

Revived or reinvigorated brands can play on nostalgia (authentic origins, with transparency) as long as they also have relevance today, but this is also not open to all-comers. We repeat that transparency is better than authenticity as a base for demonstrating usefulness. It is wise to think about your brand's future, but not to produce a long term vision in many categories, because prediction is difficult (not that we don't like difficult things), and the way people want their needs satisfied changes, individually and collectively. We are not all sailing merrily along on an ever rising tide called progress, and we re-evaluate our lives as we go through them – it is not one long road towards self-actualisation. Every twenty years or so people question and then redefine their identity (identities). [13]

For those back in the marketing departments of 1990, who forecast the explosion of the internet, texting, the iPod, and social networks? Do you want to tell us what it is all going to be like in 2025? If you are Boeing or GlaxoSmithKlein then you may have the luxury of long lead-times, but for most the future is pretty close. You can only really grow by connecting now. In moving from strategy to market, the 'Over-

Seers' - the ones with clarity of vision + wisdom need to focus on what can actually be done with the generated ideas. All too often we see intellectual virtuous circles of strategic thinking that can never result in practical executions, forever leaving managements disappointed and frustrated. Try to avoid generalisations in the same way lawyers love them. A generality to them represents a multiplication of points of interpretation, which equates to the potential to generate huge fees under the banner of establishing clarity. Pressured brand managements need to be swift and wise in the face of uncertainty. Celebrate the skill of being able to simplify challenges and deliver outstandingly on that platform. This is tougher than it seems, and great 'Simplifiers' are rare. You cannot excel at everything, a concept that many service businesses feel uncomfortable with, but which successful ones come to terms with. Be prepared to review your beliefs and perceptions in the face of unpredicted change.

This will narrow your wish-lists considerably. Redundant values stick like viruses. Let's revisit this again momentarily. Why would you list 'caring' and 'respectful of users' as values if you are in the upmarket hotel business? Would you ever practice 'uncaring' and 'disrespectful' as values? This is as bad as saying outright you are the real thing. Beware discovering you are a brand in *The Truman Show*, where your reality was known and contrived by everybody except you. 'Never knowingly undersold', a driving force behind the John Lewis Partnership retail operation in the UK for a long time expresses the attitude behind a key value. Can you same the same about your values?

How can you continue to put all this into manageable practice?

Think again about how many communication companies have managed the development of strategy so far. From the Institute of Practitioners in Advertising the advertising development process is likened to a relay race, and it comments that the initial stage is 'strategic development' including a clearly defined role for advertising to play in building a client's success.[14] This is followed by the development of a creative brief, and a creative briefing, at which the strategic understanding developed by the account management and planning team reaches the people "whose job it is to really crack the creative problem." And then there is the development of initial creative ideas. The IPA then goes on to acknowledge that many people, further along the process, will play a role in shaping a campaign, but states that it is the creative team who will originate the solution. To be fair, many agencies have recognised this as a model that was rooted in the development of television commercials as the prime creative engine, and they now issue 'Total Communication Briefs', which call for multi-media solutions, yet ideas are often still presented first around a TV-style idea. Look at the initial output from a traditional creative department to pretty much any brief, and you'll almost certainly still see that the TV commercial is alive and well, even if it doesn't get as far as the client. Why? Because that's what a lot of agency creative people were rewarded for, and continue to feel most comfortable with. A lot of ideas still follow basic narrative structures, because accepted wisdom dictates that people like great stories, so each and every brand should have one. Unfortunately great stories are not that easy to come by, especially ones that look and feel fresh, the result being the recycling of a lot of old, and not necessarily compelling ones, resulting in tired, cliché ridden advertising that does nothing to demonstrate the continuing relevance and power of the televisual medium itself. Let's hope it's not going to be a case of let's kill the medium. Using the television medium to promote brands should not be undermined by the current poor quality of much of its content.

The IPA also notes that 'the family of experts' agency structure, where a number of single discipline agencies exist under the same corporate banner, like Omnicom or WPP, in theory ought to be an ideal way of developing and managing a Total Communication Strategy. It goes on to note that this rarely happens as "in practice, the different agencies rarely communicate with each other and frequently compete against each other," [15] confirming from another source what our own experience has shown us. This is the sad reality. Everyone has their own agenda, and is looking to maximise their own share of a revenue cake. So the whole thing becomes hopelessly cost-inefficient and counter- productive.

Imagine not one planner, but six, one for each individual communications discipline, each with a slightly different proprietary tool, each one committed to persuading the client why their view is right, and obviously an improvement on the original client brief. At best intellectual chaos, at worst internecine warfare ensues.

Here is an example. Working closely with a client to develop a European launch strategy for a new product, in this case a healthy fruit-based drink, we were invited by the client to attend the first presentation of packaging ideas that the client had briefed his design agency to develop. This was not a new relationship, he and we had worked with this agency many times before, and they had been briefed to develop ideas to bring the overall European strategic brief to life. We arrived at the design agency offices to be confronted by the inevitable strategy tool, which in this instance constituted a grid designed to determine what the role of each channel, including design, should be. We spent an entire morning filling this in, before our increasingly frustrated client asked whether the agency had actually done any design work at all. The unfortunate answer was "No" because the agency felt that it needed to understand the role of all other channels before it could do the requested design work justice. In parallel the channel planning work was well in hand with a respected media agency. All the design agency had needed to do was ask for an update. Instead it chose to try to appropriate a greater share of the business for itself, no doubt hoping to gain greater input to, control over, or enhanced reputation for, the strategic development process itself. And who can blame them?

We have budgets under pressure, a greater need for new revenue streams, an increasing focus on accountability, and the demands go on. From a client perspective, this was just a waste of time and money. And there's one other point. There's a lot of talk about the desirability of media-neutrality, but in our experience there's still not enough of it around, especially from traditional agencies, because it's human nature to default back to what you feel most familiar with. Even when a common brief has been agreed, this is no guarantee of excellence across different media, even should you choose to brief all your agency partners together. We turn again to others' experience in our cause – "the faculty of different creative luminaries to interpret the same brief in utterly diverse, curiously incompatible ways and to combine this genius with a reluctance bordering on the maniacal to share work and adapt ideas from others is one of the mysteries and miseries of modern brand stewardship. The tell-tale word, and everyone in marketing has heard it, is 'interpretation'. It sounds wonderfully free, marvellously expansive, and it is, but it is the death-knell of cohesion". [16]

So, where do we go from here?

Well, we can simplify the whole process even further:

The brand owner should own the process because "he is at the centre of the spider's web". But the web is vital to survival, and how it is constructed is essential in getting results that enhance effectiveness.

Further Co-ignition – Simply The Best

Essentially, this means bringing brand owners or managers together with relevant partners, and working together over a focused time period to develop directions that have been constructed together. This can be used to develop both strategic direction for a brand, including product development and innovation, and total communication strategies.

This is not revolutionary in itself. It is effectively a distillation of workable pragmatic idea generation techniques that we have used for some time, and that work efficiently. We have been able, through experience, to finesse and hone what works most effectively in varied environments to ensure a fit with different organisation needs and cultures. We have participated in and run many such programmes whose output has ranged from new global strategies for brands to a raft of innovative ideas, subsequently executed in a range of different media and formats.

Relevant communication agency partners must be included in this process, as long as it is made clear that they are not the owners of the process, nor the sole custodians of the ensuing strategy and its executional elements, and of course, that in participating, they are committed to accepting jointly agreed outputs. We have unfortunately seen many examples of Agency participation in workshops, after which they have blithely informed the client that they have no intention of sticking with any agreements made there, because they have "after further thought, decided they no longer felt it appropriate". Changing one's mind should be done for permissible reasons, of which the 'not-invented-here' syndrome is rarely a legitimate one. There should also be key stakeholders from within the organisation who are not just in brand management, because they too need to be able to represent and promote a brand's direction and development inside the company. Indeed, our own experience of this is that involvement in the creation of new strategy and/or ideas is enormously liberating and motivating for people outside traditional marketing disciplines. They also often bring extraordinary creative thinking to the process.

The benefits of our approach are numerous:

Co-ignition:

- puts brand owners /stakeholders in the driving seat, and at the heart of the brand-building process.

- stops many of the debilitating effects of the 'not-invented-here' syndrome, If all key interested parties are involved in the process, it's not impossible, but it's often harder, for them to disagree with it afterwards, especially if the results are distilled and simple to state. Who key interested parties might be will vary from organisation to organisation, and culture to culture.

- gets people other than the marketing department involved and excited about brand development – e.g. R&D, who are often significant contributors.

- allows and forces mediated settlement between different points of view, or perspectives e.g. local market conditions vs. global overview.

- is highly involving, and creates enormous internal buy-in, and excitement.

- enables communication companies from all kinds of disciplines to buy in to a common cause and to get motivated about it. And it works when two or more agencies from the same discipline are employed in the execution of a global task.

- speeds up slow and time-consuming processes, because it utilises creativity all the way through, rather than relegating it to the final stage of 'the relay race'. Creativity then is a baton that legitimises the race, or disqualifies those who drop it.

- means that teams are finally obliged to recognise and respond to the evolving role of brands, product categories, and their relationships to users in the context of their actual lives.

Precise processes are constructed to suit the specific tasks set by the client/brand owner, and expert facilitation reduces pain quotients.

In a typical co-ignition environment, participants would include a selection of brand owners, product development people, communication agency specialists, expert observers including empowered users i.e. people who have been recruited to actively participate in the process rather than be passively observed, and anyone else who might be deemed relevant after the initial brief. Certainly, in our view, it also helps to have available some people to help express the thinking that emerges in a creative and engaging way, as well as coming up with interesting angles or perspectives. But creativity is by no means limited to creative department people. When liberated from the traditional way of doing things, we have seen many examples of people who aren't creative, deliver outstandingly creative manifestations of strategy. Imagine a stalwart of the HR department impersonating a Cockney market stall holder to deliver what he thought the philosophy of a food brand to be. Or a Senior Marketing person writing a play, as an analogy for the way in which he thought a brand should interact with its customers. We have seen these things. It's time a significant portion of idea generation was liberated from the constraints of old working models.

So, a first session would comprise an immersion phase, where all relevant information that already exists has been shared in a concise and stimulating way. This is where 'empowered users' talk about their perceptions of the brand.

However, what we also need to get at here are the points of view which are not commonly discussed. Not just issues and problems, but thoughts about where the market might be going, what consumers really think, and onwards. We call this "Let's get real". So this is also where external experts can challenge the status quo, where the group begins to discuss and debate the potential answers to the key challenges which are presented, and in particular how the internal view of the brand stacks up against the realities of its role in the lives of real people. After this it may be possible to define where a brand orbits in its product category, and in which quadrant it best sits, or should sit, should the group find our brand model a useful tool for making progress. The key objective of this session is to develop a working draft of a refreshed direction for the brand. There is then a time-out period to reflect on the output, questioning if it still makes sense, and where all key stakeholders and participants are talked to about their views and outstanding issues, their hopes, fears, and desires. A further session is convened to review the strategic thinking generated. As part of this, there is a 'What if?' challenge to the overall thinking and an invitation to the group to review this and either defeat it, accept it, or revise the thinking created to date through further iteration .The next phase is to progress to the creation of new ideas to go to market. We delegate the selection of which ideas seem to offer most potential to a voting technique in which all members of the group participate.

This flies in the face of accepted practice. It does not require that the single most highly qualified 'expert' makes the call. Instead, it involves an empowered 'group of experts' committing to getting behind making a vision that they created work. There's a big difference. It reduces 'not- invented-here' glitches and invites positive engagement. Remember that this approach does not 'condemn' people to sitting in the same place for days to work on some kind of collective 'vibe'.

At the end of the sessions all the input and output is collated and re-analysed. A further action plan is then constructed and implemented.

This is an inclusive process that is both stimulating and productive.

There's a lot to be said for Co-ignition, and for Being Simply The Best.

These days there are means to test ways forward without having to commit the whole company first.

Subjectivity in creating the destinies of many brands needs to be acknowledged and managed differently to improve value.

What drives brands are the perceptions of all the people involved in them. Job one is to pursue clarity of vision, to see clearly.

The brand owner should own the process because "he is at the centre of the spider's web". But the web is vital to survival, and how it is constructed is essential in getting results that enhance effectiveness.

Teams are finally obliged to recognise and respond to the evolving role of brands, product categories, and their relationships to users in the context of their actual lives.

13. Principles Driving Our Approach

As we have gone through our case in the book, we have highlighted certain key points or observations in the text. These have been repeated in boxes at the end of some chapters. Here we have brought them together for easy reference. Even if you read nothing else, we believe the points we expand on in our work should be being discussed, debated, and acted upon, to ensure brand and career destinies are better shaped and served, and that all those who contribute to this, in any way, are given a better chance to see how their own unique input and investment can be finessed.

Overall, in this book, we have concentrated on two things:

- the costly disconnection between subjectivity and effectiveness

- the contribution of simplification to marketing success

Here are some of the key points we introduced:

1. There is a need for a fresh perspective on what's really going on. This can unlock ways to make substantial improvements on brand investment value, returns and brand destiny.

2. We aim to demonstrate that the improved management of the perspectives people bring into the creation of brand destinies can lead to the creation of greater levels of brand performance than the current marketing models suggest.

3. If the ability to identify highly subjective perspectives and manage them diminishes, either through lack of experience or the quality of relationships with people, the fortunes of service enterprises and brands themselves will be hostages to more highly narrowcast or biased perspectives. These kill brands.

4. What is the best thing we can say about this brand today?

5. What I am saying is credible – can I justify it?

6. What kind of difference to the business will it all make?

7. What value would simplification produce?

8. It has taken generations for people to even begin to see that the role of brands is in the context of how you conduct your life in general, not in terms of how you serve the brand's view of your role in its world.

9. In many cases, looking to a product's past to discover clues about its future can only result in disappointment if its cultural role and position are not understood in the context of the major shifts in the changing role of self in defining brands today.

10. The sooner brands come to terms with the fact that they are increasingly a part of the context of people's lives, role players, bit part performers, not things that 'I' am attracted to, like iron filings to a magnet, the better the chance of building realistic connections and relationships.

11. We only really exist in the context of other things. So do Brands.

12. Brands, then, can no longer be a single thing. A brand occupies a territory, and like a quantum particle, moves about its space with many possibilities and probabilities.

13. The most successful brands are and will be the ones that understand how they can best help us to be the multiple selves we really are.

14. We tend to justify our own perspective as the real one.

15. Here are five key strategic questions we should be asking and answering:

- What does this brand do best?

- What is the most meaningful way to present your brand?

- Why should the user pay attention to the brand, on and in their terms?

- What results do you expect from brand support activity?

- How will you have prepared for the truly unexpected?

16. Many people want to be close to those who have the gift of bestowing rewards, and of showing that by taking a firm grasp of leading a team to deliver the wishes of the Bestower, they are also worthy followers and potential leaders.

17. "Would you believe this proposition yourself, and act upon it?"

18. If the subjectivity of people is a key driver of strategy, rather than it being a highly objective process, what should we do about it?

19. Our Ten Commandments:

    I. Learn what to ask, and how to ask it.
    II. Dig deep and learn to look in the right places.
    III. Don't waste time.
    IV. Work especially hard to make things simple.
    V. Test all propositions for credibility with yourself.
    VI. Encourage and respect others' contributions.
    VII. Challenge mediocrity.
    VIII. Remember how to enjoy things.
    IX. Share.
    X. Don't be frightened of saying 'I don't know, maybe you could help me understand.'

20. Where we sensibly choose to understand and accept what our users' relationships with brands really are and should or could be, new value can be recognised and released.

21. There has never been a better time to increase transparency in brands.

22. Products whose functionality is clear should get on with communicating their functional advantages, or nothing.

23. Today we live in a changed and still changing world, and in many markets we don't want or need dependent relationships with brands.

24. More people have creative potential than is generally acknowledged. It's natural. What we have to do is get better at harnessing it.

25. These days there are means to test ways forward without having to commit the whole company first.

26. Subjectivity in creating the destinies of many brands needs to be acknowledged and managed differently to improve value.

27. What drives brands are the perceptions of all the people involved in them. Job one is to pursue clarity of vision, to see clearly.

28. The brand owner should own the process because "he is at the centre of the spider's web". But the web is vital to survival, and how it is constructed is essential in getting results that enhance effectiveness.

29. Teams are finally obliged to recognise and respond to the evolving role of brands, product categories, and their relationships to users in the context of their actual lives.

14. What Goes Around...

In the late Victorian times and through the Edwardian period, if you were rich you judged the results of things more than the causes. The dining room linen needed to be clean and starched, the cutlery spotless, the food to one's taste, the wine perhaps personally selected. Basically one didn't select brands – that was the servants' job. And so it goes round.

Today, an increasing number of people use concierge services to take care of things your earning power says you don't have to. Even in recessionary periods there are people who won't give up these kinds of services. Advice may still be sought for the fine wines, but for many other things your 21st century servants will take care of it, and far more people can afford to avail themselves of these services than ever before. Not able to do that? Then you may still have acquired habits that serve you conveniently – shopping on-line, travel arrangements, banking, treats from rare suppliers in faraway places.

More and more of the successful services are following the Amazon model: 'Liked that? Try this'. Google promises to go further, probably imagining that it will be able to select brands and services for you based on your overall on-line behaviour without you needing to bother with the tedium of choice and selection, which will be in voluntary over-ride. Not listed on Google, or some other social, professional, or other service sites? – then you must be in a parallel universe called The Outside.

In 1985 one of us was invited to lunch at a small Italian restaurant in London. A pleasant gentleman described his recent work on a project that had been spun out of his company, and that he was trying to lead forward. There was not much interest from the advertising agency, largely because the product area was little known, and there was no big budget ready to be grasped. The company came to be known as Vodafone, and the gentleman was Chris Gent. In 1985, the world of *The Brand and I* didn't have space for little-known upstarts, at least not in London's West End restaurants.

Two years later the same agency had won a small piece of additional business from one of its bigger clients, Philips, who were exploring the now seeded car-based mobile-telephone business. An item was submitted for Board discussion about how a non-board director working on the client's business could possibly have an in-car phone when most of the board didn't. That reminds us nicely about focus, and of the role of subjectivity in affecting brand destiny and fortunes.

Back in 1880, in the first telephone directory in London, the new technology offered assured its wary potential subscribers or users that "there are no complicated or delicate parts in the instrument requiring any previous knowledge or care."

Trying to connect all those who affect brands and destinies isn't going to get less challenging, but at least we can try to unburden ourselves from certain constraints of the past, certain types of ingrained thinking and behaviour, and the fondness for unjustifiable complexity. Whatever experience we can share to help brands and users get the best from each other, there is no doubt that brands' destinies will still be significantly shaped by the subjective unrecorded thoughts and deeds of all those who come into contact with them. We may be able to put little spins on brand orbits, shifting some perceptions ever so slightly, but as we know from Chaos Theory, big outcomes can come from tiny changes in initial sets of conditions, and that's why we got here today. *The Brand and I* is now part of a multiverse – we can learn from a deeper understanding of it, and an ability to use the knowledge and wisdom of simplification to respond and enhance our enjoyment, use of and interaction with Brands.

Influences & Sources

Here are some of the sources that have been thought about or engaged in our approach to this work, followed by a list of many of the companies and brands that have been the roots for material or experience here, and which in turn have shaped our own perceptions, views, and ideas. Each experience and encounter involved people, and over time the numbers have grown and grown, so there are thousands who have contributed to this book, and to each and every one, whatever the nature of the encounter, thank you for contributing to this real and rich experience.

Frontispiece
'Perceptions shape decisions,' from *Enterprise Security Perception and the House of Security*, MIT, Toward Total Security Quality Management. Study, 2006

Contents

Book Structure

1. H Mintzberg, B W Ahlstrand, J Lampel, *Strategy Bites Back*, p45, Prentice Hall, FT, 2005,

Part One

The Branded World, and How I Made It So

1. It's More Subjective Than You Might Think

1. Nassim Taleb, Black Swans, Random House, 2007

2.“Personally, I don't see it that way”

3. The Impact of Personal Perspectives

1. *Financial World*, Magazine, 1993, p26

2. Richard Dawkins, *The Selfish Gene*, Oxford University Press, 1976

3. Philippe Gigantes, *Power & Greed*, p.26, 2002

4. Eric Hobsbawm, *Age of Extremes*, the Short 20th Century, Vintage Books, Feb 1996

5. D R Keogh, *The Ten Commandments for Business Failure*, Penguin 2008

6. P Rosensweig, *The Halo Effect*, Simon & Schuster, 2009

7. Charles Handy, *The Gods of Management*, Oxford University Press, 1978

8. Raymond Chandler, *The Long Goodbye*, Penguin, 1953

Challenges to Objectivity – Numbers and Knowledge

New Product Development

1. David Edgerton, *The Shock of the Old*, Profile Books, 2006

4.Living in the Real World: the Convergence of the Old and New

1. Douglas B Holt. *How Brands Become Icons*, HBS Press, 2004

2. ibid

The Creative Environment

3. George Steiner, *Grammars of Creation*, Faber and Faber, 2001

Culture, Behaviour and Expectation

1. *The Economist*, Survey on Mobile Telephony, 12 June 2007

2. Kevin Roberts, *Love Marks*, Powerhouse Books, April 2004

3. Nassim Taleb, *Fooled by Randomness*, p,240, Random House, 2004

4. John Smythe, *Observation*

5. Richard Dawkins, *The God Delusion*, p.185, First Mariner Books, 2006

6. David Copperfield, *Wasting Police Time*, Monday Books, 2006

7. Bertrand Russell, Quotation

8. T de Zengotita, *Mediated*, Bloomsbury, February, 2006

9. P Ormerod, *Why Most Things Fail*, Wiley, 2005

10. *The Times*, 3 July, p.45, 2007

11. Malcolm Gladwell, *The Tipping Point*, Little, Brown and Company, 2000

12, Richard Dawkins, *The God Delusion*, p. 361, First Mariner Books, 2006

5. Seeing the Light – Living with Diffraction

1. Daniel Kahneman & Amos Tversky, quoted in *Black Swans*, N Taleb, p191, see above note 2 Chapter 1.

2. Chris Anderson, *The Long Tail*, Hyperion, 2006

3. ibid.

4. ibid

5. *International Herald Tribune*, 23/24June, 2007

6. Strategy. Are We Asking the Wrong Questions?

1. see Book Structure 1 above

2. see It's More Subjective Than You Might Think 2 above

7. As a Client – Who Can I Turn to for the Best Advice?

1. H Mintzberg, Strategy Bites Back, see above note, in Book Structure

2. ibid

3. ibid

4. ibid.

Part Two

Brands and Reality – How to Be Simply the Best

8. Stickiness and The Power of Simplification

1. Richard Dawkins, see Chapter 3, note 2, and Chapter 4, note 5 above.

2. P Rosensweig, *The Halo Effect*, Simon & Schuster, 2009

3. John Kay, *The Long and Short of It*, p.74–78, Erasmus Press, 2009.

4. ibid

5. J M Keynes, Quotation.

6. ibid 3

9. A Simpler Way to Work with Brands More Effectively

10. Predictable Barriers to Keeping It Simple

1. John Roberts, *The Modern Firm*, Oxford University Press, 2004

2. Joseph Jaffe, *Life after the 30:Spot,* John Wiley & Sons, 2005

3. Reference to a Folger's Coffee US print ad.

11. Language & Structure – New Perspectives

12. Co-Ignition – Getting More With Less

1. The Doors, *Light My Fire*, CD Album, The Doors, 1967

2. Derek Day & Helen Edwards, *Creating Passion Brands*, p.52, Kogan Page, 2007

3. S Zuboff & J Maxmin, *The Support Economy*, p.101, October 2002

4. T de Zengotita, *Mediated*, p.77 et al., 2005

5. William Henry Davies (1871–1994), *Leisure,* Poem

6. J Gilmore & B Joseph Pine, *Authenticity*, p.44, Wiley, 2009

7. Cass R Sunstein, *Infotopia*, p.65-69, Oxford University Press, 2006

8. Andrew Keen, *The Cult of the Amateur*, p.83, Doubleday, 2007

9. N Ind & R Bjerke, *Branding Governance*, Kogan Page, 2007

10. Denison & Mishra, *Organisation Sciences,* 6, p.204–23

11. P Rosensweig, *The Halo Effect,* p.31, Simon & Schuster, 2009

12. Harvard Business School, Clayton Christensen

13. "Center for Cultural Studies and Analysis", Margaret King

14. IPA, *Excellence in Advertising*, p.13 et al., Elsevier, 1999

15. ibid, Chap, "Total Communications Strategy", p.240

16. *Passion Brands*, see note 2 above, pp.217–18

13. Principles Driving Our Approach

14. What Goes Around...

Companies: Material and Experience Sources:

Access Credit Cards	Allied Breweries
Barclays	Basset Confectionery
Blockbuster Video	Bradford & Bingley Building Society
British Airways	British Gas
British Midland	Bucherer
Cadbury Schweppes	Citroen
COI	Colman's
Colgate Palmolive	Conde Nast
Coral Leisure Group	Coty
Danish Agricultural Producers	Danone
DMB&B	Dupont
EuroRSCG	States of Guernsey
Everest Double Glazing	Foote Cone & Belding
F W Woolworth	Hewlett Packard
Holiday Inn	HP Foods
ICI	
IDC	Johnson & Johnson,
Kodak	Kraft General Foods
Margaret Astor	M&G Unit Trusts
Mars	Mercedes Benz
National Dairy Council	Nestle
NOP	Orange Telecom
Pirelli	Procter & Gamble
Reckitt Benckiser	Rimmel
Royal Dutch Philips Electronics	Suchard
Somerfield	The Sunday Times
Unilever	Unisys
Volvo	Wine Institute of California
WPP	Wyeth Nutrition
Xerox